D0104338

CALM ANSWERS *for a* CONFUSED CHURCH
A STUDY OF 1 CORINTHIANS 12–16

BIBLE STUDY GUIDE

From the Bible-teaching ministry of

Charles R. Swindoll

INSIGHT FOR LIVING

Charles R. Swindoll is a graduate of Dallas Theological Seminary and has served in pastorates for more than twenty-five years, including churches in Texas, New England, and California. Since 1971 he has served as senior pastor of the First Evangelical Free Church of Fullerton, California. Chuck's radio program, "Insight for Living," began in 1979. In addition to his church and radio ministries, Chuck enjoys writing. He has authored numerous books and booklets on a variety of subjects.

This guide is the third in a three-part series on the book of 1 Corinthians. Based on the outlines of Chuck's sermons, the study guide text is coauthored by Julie Martin, a graduate of Biola University. The Living Insights are written by Bill Butterworth, a graduate of Florida Bible College, Dallas Theological Seminary, and Florida Atlantic University. Julie Martin is an associate editor in the Educational Products Department at Insight for Living, and Bill Butterworth is currently a staff writer in the Educational Products Department.

Editor in Chief:	Cynthia Swindoll
Coauthor of Text:	Julie Martin
Author of Living Insights:	Bill Butterworth
Editorial Assistant:	Glenda Schlahta
Copy Manager:	Jac La Tour
Senior Copy Editor:	Jane Gillis
Copy Editor:	Wendy Peterson
Director, Communications Division:	Carla Beck
Project Manager:	Nina Paris
Project Supervisor:	Cassandra Clark
Art Director:	Donna Mayo
Production Artists:	Steve Cox and Diana Vasquez
Typographer:	Bob Haskins
Cover Photographer:	Tom Grill/Comstock Inc.
Print Production Manager:	Deedee Snyder
Printer:	Frye and Smith

ISBN 0-8499-8400-9

Ordering Information

An album that contains sixteen messages on eight cassettes and corresponds to this study guide may be purchased through the Sales Department of Insight for Living, Post Office Box 4444, Fullerton, California 92634. For ordering information and a current catalog, please write our office or call (714) 870-9161.

Canadian residents may obtain a catalog and ordering information through Insight for Living Ministries, Post Office Box 2510, Vancouver, British Columbia, Canada V6B 3W7, (604) 272-5811. Australian residents should direct their correspondence to Insight for Living Ministries, General Post Office Box 2823 EE, Melbourne, Victoria 3001. Other overseas residents should direct their correspondence to our Fullerton office.

If you wish to order by Visa or MasterCard, you are welcome to use our toll-free number, (800) 772-8888, Monday through Friday, between the hours of 8:30 A.M. and 4:00 P.M., Pacific time. This number may be used anywhere in the United States except Alaska, California, and Hawaii. Orders from these areas can be made by calling our general office number, (714) 870-9161. Orders from Canada can be made by calling (604) 272-5811.

Table of Contents

*This message was not a part of the original series but is compatible with it.

Calm Answers
for a Confused Church
A Study of 1 Corinthians 12–16

Few things are worse than being confused, especially when it comes to confusion over spiritual issues. The Corinthian Christians were in just such a condition when Paul wrote this letter. They found themselves in disagreement, which led to their developing cliques and splinter groups—each going in a different direction, listening to a different leader. Our adversary loves to find churches immobilized by those conditions!

In this last section of Paul's letter, we'll discover numerous insights into major areas of struggle. Woven through the fabric of these lessons is God's concern that we not allow divisions to break down our love for each other. How easy it is to forget that fact! There are many more things that hold us together than separate us as children of the living God.

My hope, as we study the final five chapters of this grand letter, is that you will realize anew how relevant, how timely, and how helpful God's Word really is. It does indeed live and abide forever.

Chuck Swindoll

Putting Truth into Action

Knowledge apart from application falls short of God's desire for His children. Knowledge must result in change and growth. Consequently, we have constructed this Bible study guide with these purposes in mind: (1) to stimulate discovery, (2) to increase understanding, and (3) to encourage application.

At the end of each lesson is a section called **Living Insights.** There you'll be given assistance in further Bible study, and you'll be encouraged to contemplate and apply the things you've learned. This is the place where the lesson is fitted with shoe leather for your walk through the varied experiences of life.

It's our hope that you'll discover numerous ways to use this tool. Some useful avenues we suggest are personal meditation, joint discovery, and discussion with your spouse, family, work associates, friends, or neighbors. The study guide is also practical for Sunday school classes, Bible study groups, and, of course, as a study aid for the "Insight for Living" radio broadcast.

In order to derive the greatest benefit from this process, we suggest that you record your responses to the lessons in the space which has been provided for you. In view of the kinds of questions asked, your study guide may become a journal filled with your many discoveries and commitments. We anticipate that you will find yourself returning to it periodically for review and encouragement.

Julie Martin
Coauthor of Text

Bill Butterworth
Author of Living Insights

CALM ANSWERS *for a* CONFUSED CHURCH

A STUDY OF 1 CORINTHIANS 12–16

One Head, One Body, Many Functions

1 Corinthians 12:1–11

Listening to Handel's "Water Music" on your home stereo and hearing it performed live at the symphony are two entirely different experiences.

The sounds may be exactly the same—the same bravura entrances, legato strains, even the same soundful silence between movements. But our awareness of the conductor, the orchestra, and the separate instruments is diminished when the music's only visible source is a needle reading the spinning vinyl grooves of a record. There's something about *seeing* the music happen that creates a sense of wonder and understanding.

At the symphony, you see the entire orchestra assembled as a whole, as well as each individual musician, plus the black-tie conductor, who seems to pull the music from the belly of each instrument with a sweep of the baton.

Similarly, understanding how spiritual gifts work euphoniously in a church body takes more than just listening to the harmony the members make when tuned in to their gifts. It takes seeing each believer as an individual instrument, as vital to the body, as directed by God.

I. Some Crucial Clarifications

Before we begin our study, let's clarify the difference between the *gift, fruit,* and *gifts* of the Spirit—a distinction that often becomes muddled in our minds.

A. The gift of the Spirit. Given the moment a person believes in Christ, this gift is the Holy Spirit Himself (see John 14:16–17, Luke 11:13, 1 Cor. 3:16). It's a gift that's given *to* us—it has no receipt; it can never be returned.

B. The fruit of the Spirit. The fruit of the Spirit is revealed in character qualities, virtues produced *within* us—"love, joy, peace, patience, kindness, goodness, faithfulness, gentleness, self-control" (Gal. 5:22–23a). The Spirit plants the seeds in all

1

believers so that each of us has the ability to produce every kind of fruit—the whole orchard!

C. **The gifts of the Spirit.** Carried out *through* us, spiritual gifts are skills and abilities, instruments God gives us to benefit the whole body. Not to be prayed for or earned, our spiritual gifts are natural for us to play—ones we are thrilled and excited to practice.

Sharing Your Gifts with Pleasure and Ease

For someone who possesses the gift of mercy, showing compassion to another is almost as natural as breathing. And for someone with the gift of teaching, there's nothing as exciting as facing a group of people who are eager to learn.

Using your gift, whatever it is, should bless not only others but *you,* because your gift will allow you to express your personality and deepest desires. Ray Stedman emphasizes this point in his book *Body Life.*

> The exercise of a spiritual gift is always a satisfying, enjoyable experience.... Jesus said it was his constant delight to do the will of the one who sent him. The Father's gift awakened his own desire and he went about doing what he intensely enjoyed doing.[1]

II. A Practical Exposition

In 1 Corinthians 12:1–11, Paul gives us a solid understanding of spiritual gifts. He focuses not so much on the gifts themselves, but on how and why the gifts together produce a full, real-life sound, rich in harmony.

A. **Introduction.** Paul begins by stamping the issue of spiritual gifts Important!

> Now concerning spiritual gifts, brethren, I do not want you to be unaware. (v. 1)

Unaware comes from the Greek word *agnoeō,* which means "not knowable" or "not known." Our word *agnostic* comes from the same root. Paul felt it was crucial for believers to be aware of the subject—that when it comes to discovering and exercising the spiritual gifts God has given us, there's no place for ignorance.

---

1. Ray C. Stedman, *Body Life,* 2d ed., rev. (Glendale, Calif.: Regal Books, 1977), p. 56.

B. Digression. Paul preludes his main discussion with a pertinent reminder:

> You know that when you were pagans, you were led astray to the dumb idols, however you were led. Therefore I make known to you, that no one speaking by the Spirit of God says, "Jesus is accursed"; and no one can say, "Jesus is Lord," except by the Holy Spirit. (vv. 2–3)

Before we were saved, we were without the Spirit. But now, we who confess Jesus as Lord can be sure the Spirit lives in us. And we can count on Him to draw out the gifts that are deep within us with His thundering, velvet hand.

C. Instruction. Making beautiful music takes more than just practice. It requires knowing the theory behind the notes on the page—understanding chord progressions, scales, and rhythms. Likewise, being fully aware of our spiritual gifts requires not only that we understand how to perform our gifts excellently but also that we know their source, the reason behind them, what they are, and who they're given to.

1. **The source of spiritual gifts.** In verses 4–6, Paul reveals our gift giver.

> Now there are varieties of gifts, but the same *Spirit.* And there are varieties of ministries, and the same *Lord.* And there are varieties of effects, but the same *God* who works all things in all persons. (emphasis added)

"There are varieties of gifts," says Paul. Various gifts having various ministries having various results. *But,* as Paul says, there is "the same Spirit . . . the same Lord . . . the same God" who produces them all. Notice that the entire Godhead is involved in the gift giving. Spiritual gifts are so important to God that He involves His whole self in giving them.

2. **The purpose of spiritual gifts.** In verse 7, Paul rings out the rich truth of why God gives us spiritual gifts:

> But to each one is given the manifestation of the Spirit for the common good.

God has spiritually gifted *each one* of us. In the same way that every member of an orchestra plays an instrument, each member of God's family has been given spiritual gifts—gifts that, when exercised, manifest the Holy Spirit. Why? "For the common good." Derived from the Greek word *sumpherō,* this phrase means "to bring together, to lift up." God doesn't intend us to practice our spiritual instruments alone in insulated, soundproof rooms. He wants us to take our seats in the orchestra and, under the Spirit's direction, make music that builds others up . . . a sweet, sweet sound in God's ears.

No Part Too Small

Most of us would admit that we have been given some kind of spiritual gift. But some think that their gift is insignificant, like the trickle of a piccolo in a downpour of brassy blasts and thundering timpani claps.

Just remember, there is no part too small. You may not carry the melody or set the rhythm for the rest of the orchestra, but without your part the sound won't be as full and harmonious. Without your part, the sound will always be less than completely beautiful.

---

3. **The identity of spiritual gifts.** In verses 8–10, Paul identifies the spiritual gifts:

> For to one is given the word of wisdom through the Spirit, and to another the word of knowledge according to the same Spirit; to another faith by the same Spirit, and to another gifts of healing by the one Spirit, and to another the effecting of miracles, and to another prophecy, and to another the distinguishing of spirits, to another various kinds of tongues, and to another the interpretation of tongues.

Based on this passage and others (Rom. 12:6–8, Eph. 4:11, 1 Pet. 4:11), we can sort the spiritual gifts into the following categories:[2]

Support Gifts	Service Gifts	Sign Gifts
Apostleship	Administrations	Distinguishing of spirits
Prophecy	Exhortation	Miracles
Evangelism	Faith	Healings
Pastor-Teacher	Giving	Tongues
Teaching	Helps	Interpretation of tongues
	Showing mercy	

---

2. From the study guide *Spiritual Gifts,* coauthored by Ken Gire, from the Bible-teaching ministry of Charles R. Swindoll (Fullerton, Calif.: Insight for Living, 1986), p. 7.

4. **The distribution of spiritual gifts.** Like a conductor who hands out the score to the musicians before a performance, the Spirit distributes His gifts to all believers.

> But one and the same Spirit works all these things, distributing to each one individually just as He wills. (1 Cor. 12:11)

He distributes our gifts, not because we work, pray, or plead for them, but *just as He wills.* He selects our gifts for us personally, tailoring them to our personality and desires.

III. Some Timeless Applications

Learning music theory is never an end in itself. Its goal is to be used with an instrument—practiced and perfected. Here's some "spiritual gift theory" that will help enhance your performance in the body of Christ.

A. **Being aware of your spiritual gift is pleasing to God.** God does not want us to be ignorant about spiritual gifts (see v. 1). So study them closely, and discover which ones allow you to express your personality and desires.[3]

B. **Being willing to use your gift is constructive to the whole body of Christ.** When you use your gift, everyone is blessed. The sound of your spiritual instrument reaches every ear.

C. **Being satisfied with your gift is an honor to its giver.** You will never bring as much glory to God as when you are exercising the gifts He has given you. Don't long for the gifts you *don't* have, but rejoice in the ones you do.

A Final Thought

You can sit in the back pew with your arms folded, listening to the rest of your church body play their spiritual instruments. But why should you listen, uninvolved and from a distance, when you have an important part to play— a part nobody else can play but you?

Remember, if you refuse to use your gift, your fellow believers miss out on some important "building up"... and God misses out on some of the glory He so rightly deserves.

> As each one has received a special gift, employ it in serving one another, as good stewards of the manifold grace of God. Whoever speaks, let him speak, as it were, the utterances of God; whoever serves, let him do so as by the strength

---

3. For some help in your exploration, see "The Discovery of Your Gift" in William J. McRae's book *The Dynamics of Spiritual Gifts* (Grand Rapids, Mich.: Zondervan Publishing House, 1976), pp. 103–19.

which God supplies; so that in all things God may be glorified through Jesus Christ, to whom belongs the glory and dominion forever and ever. *Amen.* (1 Pet. 4:10–11, emphasis added)

 Living Insights

Study One ▬▬▬▬▬▬▬▬▬▬▬▬▬▬▬▬▬▬▬▬▬▬▬▬▬▬

We have titled this section of 1 Corinthians, chapters 12–16, *Calm Answers for a Confused Church.* A casual reading of the text will reveal both the confusion of the church and the calmness of the answers.

● Read 1 Corinthians 12–16. Using the chart that's provided, look for statements on both the confusion within the church and the answers given. Jot them down in the appropriate column.

Calm Answers for a Confused Church	
Confusion Expressed	Answers Given

Living Insights

Because of the variety of spiritual gifts, believers may express them-selves in many different ways. Have you given any attention to your gifts recently? Take a few minutes to answer the following questions.

• What are your gifts? _____

_____

_____

• How do you put them to use? _____

_____

_____

• When are you most satisfied with your gifts? _____

_____

_____

• When are you most dissatisfied with your gifts? _____

_____

_____

• If you could give one piece of advice concerning gifts, what would it be?

_____

_____

_____

Analogies from Anatomy
1 Corinthians 12:12–31a

In 1898, John Milton Gregory was buried on the campus of the University of Illinois—where he gave thirteen years of his life teaching and administrating. A hall has since been built and named after him in honor of the unique gifts he shared with the university, now one of the finest schools in the northern Midwest.

Gregory, however, left in his legacy a facet of his life far more significant than his tombstone and the hall that bears his name. Shortly before his death, he wrote a book titled *The Seven Laws of Teaching*.

In this book, Gregory profoundly, yet simply, laid down teaching's seven laws. The third one is particularly relevant to our study.

The *language* used as a *medium* between teacher and learner must be *common* to both.[1]

We've all had teachers we wished would have read Gregory's book— teachers who delighted in displaying their vocabulary and knowledge, but were not really interested in whether or not we understood them.

Then there was Jesus, the master teacher, who instinctively knew Gregory's law long before it was ever put into print. When explaining profound, unfathomable truth, Jesus used common language. He talked of shepherds and sheep, vines and branches, a door, a light, daily bread.

Following in the footsteps of the Lord Jesus is the apostle Paul. In 1 Corinthians 12:12–31a, he explains the hard-to-grasp truth about the unity and diversity of the Body of Christ using an analogy common to us all—the human body.

I. Many Parts, One Unit

Instead of getting into a dry, theological discussion, Paul explains the spiritual oneness of the Body of Christ by likening it to the union of the parts of our physical bodies.

For even as the body is one and yet has many members, and all the members of the body, though they are many, are one body, so also is Christ. (v. 12)

From the tops of our hard skulls to the soft soles of our feet, each part of our bodies, though diverse, is united as a whole. Likewise, every member of Christ's Church is part of the same unit. Paul tells us why in verses 13–14:

---

1. John Milton Gregory, *The Seven Laws of Teaching*, rev. ed. (1917; reprint, Grand Rapids, Mich.: Baker Book House, 1954), p. 19.

For by one Spirit we were all baptized into one body, whether Jews or Greeks, whether slaves or free, and we were all made to drink of one Spirit.[2] For the body is not one member, but many.

It is because of the Holy Spirit's ministry that we are all part of the same unit. From a young man in southern Indonesia, to a lady in the depths of Hong Kong's inner city, to the sweetest old saint in northern Canada, all believers are members of the same Body because we all have been baptized by the Holy Spirit.

A Note of Clarification

Unfortunately, in the Church today the teaching of the baptism of the Holy Spirit has become a battleground of confusion rather than a doctrine of clarity.

We are commanded to be *filled* with the Holy Spirit, but being *baptized* by the Spirit is not our responsibility. When we put our trust in Christ, the Holy Spirit baptizes us, permanently changing our identity from Satan's family to God's.[3]

II. Many Parts, Each Important

Next, Paul builds on his analogy, and with imagination and humor he illustrates the significance of each believer in the Body.

A. The parts. Suppose that our feet and our ears, body parts that aren't particularly attractive, could talk.

If the foot says, "I am not a part of the body because I am not a hand," that does not make it any less a part of the body. And what would you think if you heard an ear say, "I am not part of the body because I am only an ear, and not an eye"? Would that make it any less a part of the body? (vv. 15–16)[4]

---

2. According to David Prior, the word *baptized* "carries the double connotation of 'being initiated into' and 'being overwhelmed by'. For example, contemporary secular Greek sources spoke of a submerged ship being 'baptized'. That ship was not merely 'initiated into' water; it was thoroughly 'overwhelmed by' water. Indeed, we can go on to say that it was 'made to drink of' the water: *i.e.* the water was inside the ship as well as the ship being underneath the water. Paul seems, then, to be saying both that Christians are in the Holy Spirit, and that the Holy Spirit is in Christians, parallel to our being in Christ and Christ being in us." From *The Message of 1 Corinthians: Life in the Local Church* (Downers Grove, Ill.: InterVarsity Press, 1985), p. 211.

3. For more information on the baptism of the Holy Spirit, see the chapter "The Baptizing Work of the Holy Spirit" in *The Holy Spirit,* by Charles Caldwell Ryrie (Chicago, Ill.: Moody Press, 1965), pp. 74–79.

4. The Living Bible (Wheaton, Ill.: Tyndale House Publishers, 1971).

Even though big ears and filthy feet are less appealing than clean hands and bright, sparkling eyes, they are still vital to the body. In the same way, every member of the Body of Christ performs a significant function for the entire Body.

B. The whole. In verse 17, Paul shows the absurdity of a body composed of only one member.

> Suppose the whole body were an eye—then how would you hear? Or if your whole body were just one big ear, how could you smell anything?[5]

Picture it. A body that's one huge ear—no sense of smell, no sight, no taste. It would probably hear great! But without the other members, it wouldn't be of much use.

C. The design. God didn't create bodies that have only one function, for they would be grotesque and not really bodies at all (v. 19). Similarly, He didn't design the Church to have members who possess the same spiritual gifts, but He "has placed the members, each one of them, in the body, just as He desired" (v. 18).

Combating Comparison

If you've been gifted as a foot, it's easy to look at those gifted as hands and think how skilled, how capable they are, and that you're not important at all. That's exactly what the enemy wants you to think. He'll do anything he can to get you to stay in your shoe!

But the truth is that, in its perfect design, the Body of Christ is dependent on each part—feet, ears, hands, as well as organs that are never seen—to be healthy.

Don't let Satan shelve your self-worth in a shoe box or sell you the idea that you aren't important. Remember that each part is important.

That means *you*.

III. Many Parts, All Interdependent

In a healthy body of believers, all the members depend on each other, lean on each other, and help each other function at their best.

A. No room for a spirit of independence. Paul continues his analogy:

> The eye can never say to the hand, "I don't need you." The head can't say to the feet, "I don't need you."

---

5. The Living Bible.

And some of the parts that seem weakest and least important are really the most necessary. Yes, we are especially glad to have some parts that seem rather odd! And we carefully protect from the eyes of others those parts that should not be seen, while of course the parts that may be seen do not require this special care. So God has put the body together in such a way that extra honor and care are given to those parts that might otherwise seem less important. (vv. 21–24)[6]

An eye may be able to see a hurt child, but it could never reach out to comfort the child like a hand could. And a head wouldn't have much information to process if the feet didn't carry it around, letting it experience the life around it. In the same way, some members in the Body of Christ seem insignificant on the surface. But like the tiny anvil bones of the inner ear that hold part of the secret to the world of hearing, they are desperately needed by the other members.

B. A case for interdependence. In verses 25–26, Paul explains why God has created us to be interdependent.

That there should be no division in the body, but that the members should have the same care for one another. And if one member suffers, all the members suffer with it; if one member is honored, all the members rejoice with it.

Infected tonsils affect more than just your throat; they affect the way your entire body feels. You can't eat, sing, talk, or sleep. But just as the whole body suffers when one member is sick, so it is rejuvenated when that member is restored to health.

Showing Your Dark Side

As Mark Twain said, "Everyone is a moon, and has a dark side which he never shows to anybody."[7] We are afraid to be transparent, vulnerable, afraid to admit that we have a weakness or a need.

What about you? Do you show your dark side to others, or keep it safely hidden out of everyone's view?

To help illuminate your level of vulnerability, consider these four questions: (1) Within the last month, did you express to someone else an area of need in your life?

---

6. The Living Bible.

7. *Bartlett's Familiar Quotations,* 14th ed., rev. and enl. (Boston, Mass.: Little, Brown and Co., 1968), p. 763.

(2) Within the last month, did you express gratitude to another member of the Body for what that person means to you? (3) Would the sign No Help Wanted fit around your neck? (4) If someone asked, "How can I help you this week?" would you be embarrassed or offended?

Usually, that side of our lives is dark only because we've kept it hidden, out of the warm light of forgiveness and acceptance. Won't you dare depend on that light, light that others in the Body are waiting to give you?

IV. Many Parts, None Exclusive

Next, Paul emphasizes the spiritual side of his analogy, explaining that there is no such thing as an exclusive gift in the Body of Christ. The Corinthians had inflated the value of the gift of tongues. They made it the *sine qua non* of spirituality, the single evidence that one possessed the Holy Spirit. So Paul sets them straight.

All are not apostles, are they? All are not prophets, are they? All are not teachers, are they? All are not workers of miracles, are they? All do not have gifts of healings, do they? All do not speak with tongues, do they? All do not interpret, do they? (vv. 29–30)

In verses 27–28, Paul makes it clear that no single gift is all-important, and that if you were to put differing gifts on a scale, they wouldn't necessarily weigh in evenly. Notice the order in which he lists the gifts:

Now you are Christ's body, and individually members of it. And God has appointed in the church, *first* apostles, *second* prophets, *third* teachers, *then* miracles, *then* gifts of healings, helps, administrations, various kinds of tongues. (emphasis added)

Paul explains that just as no human body is exclusively an eye, so Christ's Body isn't composed of people who possess the same gift.

V. Many Parts, Some Greater

In closing, Paul urges us to "earnestly desire the greater gifts" (v. 31a). The greater gifts, such as prophecy and teaching, build up the whole Body. The lesser gifts, such as tongues, build up only a small part (see 14:1–5). So, as Christians, we should pursue the exercising of the greater gifts, with the building up of the whole Body in mind.

┌─ *The Language of Love* ─────────────────────────────

Like John Milton Gregory, who believed in communicating with common, analogous language, God has communicated His love for us in His own perfect language of love (see John 3:16, Rom. 5:8, 1 John 3:1a).

God doesn't talk about His love for us in high-flown, erudite terms. He sent His Son—the Word made flesh . . . a living, breathing analogy—to die that we might truly understand how much He values us.

 ## Living Insights

Study One

In education, it's easy to see the advantages of using analogy. Analogies allow a teacher to convey abstract concepts through concrete examples. In 1 Corinthians 12:12–31a, Paul brings the concepts of unity and diversity alive through the use of the human body.

- Let's examine this passage of Scripture in greater detail. A very successful way to get to the heart of the text is to paraphrase the verses. Paraphrasing is the art of rewriting the verses in your own words. This allows the student of Scripture to express greater meanings and bring out some of the feelings that are underneath the words of the text. Try your hand at this art by paraphrasing this passage.

1 Corinthians 12:12–31a

_____

_____

_____

_____

_____

_____

_____

_____

_____

_____

_____

Continued on next page

_____

_____

_____

_____

_____

_____

_____

🌳 *Living Insights*

From this study one thing is clear: there are many parts to the Body of Christ. Take the main points of this lesson and apply them to people in the Body that you know.

- The Body of Christ is one unit, yet many parts. List the people you know who represent different parts.

_____

_____

_____

- Now write down how each of those members is important to the Body.

_____

_____

_____

- How are they all interdependent? _____

_____

_____

- Why isn't each part exclusive? _____

_____

_____

Love: The Greatest of All
1 Corinthians 13

Although one of the most majestic wonders of the world, the Grand Canyon is actually a monument to death.

This chasm, the deepest on the earth's surface, lies virtually lifeless, except for an occasional juniper tree or tuft of low scrub. And almost all the other signs of life are of life now gone, life since fossiled into the limestone and sandstone of the canyon's crusty cliffs.

As in northern Arizona, so in all our hearts there's a yawning cleft where love originally was to have mountained but was eroded by a ruthless river of snaking selfishness and sin.

There are times when we are made especially aware of our loveless canyon. Times when we give our marriage vows a Judas kiss, give stones to someone who asks us for bread, or thoughtlessly slice another's self-esteem with a razor-blade tongue.

But we aren't without hope. Even as a lack of love can create a deep and lifeless canyon in our hearts, the presence of love, the greatest gift of all, can bridge it.

In 1 Corinthians 13, Paul gives the blueprints for this bridge. We'll approach this passage neither technically nor critically; we'll focus not so much on being informed, but on being transformed.

I. Love's Essential Presence

In verses 1–3, Paul explains just how essential love is to our lives, showing us that without it, the gifts we pedestal are worthless.

> If I speak with the tongues of men and of angels, but do not have love, I have become a noisy gong or a clanging cymbal. And if I have the gift of prophecy, and know all mysteries and all knowledge; and if I have all faith, so as to remove mountains, but do not have love, I am nothing. And if I give all my possessions to feed the poor, and if I deliver my body to be burned, but do not have love, it profits me nothing.

The presence of love is so vital that without it, the most eloquent, impressive speech would sound like a cacophonous clang. Without it, prophecy, knowledge, faith are nothing. And the most unselfish, sacrificial acts are worthless.

II. Love's Basic Qualities

After explaining the matchless value of love, Paul gives us a clear, poetic description of what love is made of—a description we can't help but respond to.

> Love is so patient and so kind;
> Love never boils with jealousy;
> It never boasts, is never puffed with pride;
> It does not act with rudeness, or insist upon its rights;
> It never gets provoked, it never harbors evil thoughts;
> Is never glad when wrong is done,
> But always glad when truth prevails;
> It bears up under anything,
> It exercises faith in everything,
> It keeps up hope in everything,
> It gives us power to endure in anything.[1]

III. Love's Eternal Endurance

In verse 8, Paul adds one final characteristic of love to the list: "Love never fails."

A. The everlasting virtue. At first blush, the fact that love never fails suggests that love will never let you down. But in

---

1. Charles B. Williams, *The New Testament in the Language of the People* (Chicago, Ill.: Moody Press, 1966), p. 381.

16

Greek, the word *fail* means "to fall, to collapse, to come to an end, to be terminated." The idea, then, is that love, unlike a mountain eroded by the elements, will never collapse, never fade, never end. It survives everything—invincible love! Shakespeare speaks of the enduring quality of love in one of his most moving sonnets.

Love is not love
Which alters when it alteration finds,
Or bends with the remover to remove.
O no, it is an ever-fixed mark
That looks on tempests and is never shaken;
It is the star to every wand'ring bark,
Whose worth's unknown, although his highth be
taken. . . .
Love alters not with his brief hours and weeks,
But bears it out even to the edge of doom.[2]

B. The temporary gifts. Juxtaposed to love are three gifts that *will* fade away.

But if there are gifts of prophecy, they will be done away; if there are tongues, they will cease; if there is knowledge, it will be done away. For we know in part, and we prophesy in part; but when the perfect comes, the partial will be done away. (vv. 8b–10)

The "perfect" refers to the Lord Jesus' Second Coming. When we see Him face-to-face, our wonder will be unshackled; our knowledge will be complete. The apostle John explains this in 1 John 3:2.

Beloved, now we are children of God, and it has not appeared as yet what we shall be. We know that, when He appears, we shall be like Him, because we shall see Him just as He is.

C. Two vivid illustrations. Paul illustrates this truth with two familiar examples.

When I was a child, I used to speak as a child, think as a child, reason as a child; when I became a man, I did away with childish things. (1 Cor. 13:11)

Until the Lord comes, we will speak, think, and reason as children. But when He does come, our understanding will be mature, complete. Adding to his point, Paul writes,

---

2. William Shakespeare, "Sonnet 116" in *The Riverside Shakespeare,* G. Blakemore Evans, ed. (Boston, Mass.: Houghton Mifflin Co., 1974), p. 1770.

For now we see in a mirror[3] dimly,[4] but then face to face; now I know in part, but then I shall know fully just as I also have been fully known. (v. 12)

When the Lord comes, the distorted images of reality, the mysteries, the riddles will all be gone. When we see the Savior face-to-face, our question marks will all be changed to exclamation points!

IV. Love's Preeminent Role

In verse 13, Paul declares that love is greater than all other virtues.

But now abide faith, hope, love, these three; but the greatest of these is love.

Why? Because "faith without love is cold, and hope without love is grim. Love is the fire which kindles faith and love is the light which turns hope into certainty."[5] Also, when faith and hope become visible, faith will be replaced by sight, and hope replaced by possession. Only love will remain. Because God Himself *is* love.

V. Love's Consistent Exhibition

None of us have completed building the bridge of love in our lives, and we never will until we're in the presence of the only model of perfect love. However, as long as we live, we're to pursue love with everything we've got. The following questions will help you see how far you are in your bridge-building process—and how far you've yet to go.

A. Do you consider love absolutely essential? Is love the most important aspect in your relationships with others? Is loving others your daily objective and goal?

B. Do you express your love? It's difficult for many of us to show our love to others, especially when we've been burned in giving it without reservation. Even though it may be risky, do you say "I love you"; do you give that hug? Do you *show* others how much you love them?

C. Does your love fade in and out? Even though loving isn't always easy, it must be unconditional. Does your love turn from hot to cold depending on the actions of others? Or is your love something they can count on no matter how undeserving they might be?

---

3. "Findlay writes: 'Ancient mirrors made of burnished metal—a specialty of Corinth—were poor reflectors; the art of silvering glass was discovered in the 13th century.'" From *Word Meanings in the New Testament,* by Ralph Earle (Grand Rapids, Mich.: Baker Book House, 1986), p. 239.

4. From the Greek word translated *dimly,* we get our word *enigma.*

5. William Barclay, *The Letters to the Corinthians,* 2d ed., The Daily Study Bible Series (Philadelphia, Pa.: Westminster Press, 1956), p. 140.

D. Does love come to the surface of your life more often than any other virtue? If those around you were to choose one virtue to describe you, would it be love?

> ┌─ *The Greatest Source of Love* ─────────────
> The ability to love can only come from love's source. So as we try to bridge the loveless canyon in our hearts, let's recall afresh the great love God has shown us through the Lord Jesus—that we may be filled with His love to share with others.
>
> Never shall my soul forget those chambers of fellowship where Thou hast unveiled Thyself to me. Had Moses his cleft in the rock, where he saw the train, the back parts of his God? We, too, have had our clefts in the rock, where we have seen the full splendours of the Godhead in the person of Christ.... Precious Lord Jesus, give us a fresh draught of Thy wondrous love.[6]

 Living Insights

Study One ■■■

Our study now brings us to one of the most familiar passages in the Bible. Many of us even know this text from memory. Let's take a further look into the *meaning* behind the words.

● In the list below, we've paraphrased the characteristics of love found in 1 Corinthians 13. Try to find more shades of meaning within the text itself; then expand on these with the help of a Bible dictionary. After discovering the meaning, jot down some other passages that address these specific traits.

Love Is . . .

Patient

Expanded definition: _____

_____

_____

6. Charles H. Spurgeon, *Morning and Evening: Daily Readings* (McLean, Va.: MacDonald Publishing Co., n.d.), p. 65.

Additional texts: _____

_____

Kind

Expanded definition: _____

_____

_____

Additional texts: _____

_____

Not Jealous

Expanded definition: _____

_____

_____

Additional texts: _____

_____

Not Boastful

Expanded definition: _____

_____

_____

Additional texts: _____

_____

Humble

Expanded definition: _____

_____

_____

Additional texts: _____

_____

Courteous

Expanded definition: _____

_____

_____

Additional texts: _____

_____

Unselfish

Expanded definition: _____

_____

_____

Additional texts: _____

_____

Not Provoked

Expanded definition: _____

_____

_____

Additional texts: _____

_____

Free of Grudges

Expanded definition: _____

_____

_____

Additional texts: _____

_____

Grieved at Sin

Expanded definition: _____

_____

Continued on next page

Additional texts: _____

Always Rejoicing with the Truth

Expanded definition: _____

_____

Additional texts: _____

Steadfast

Expanded definition: _____

_____

Additional texts: _____

Affirming

Expanded definition: _____

_____

Additional texts: _____

Hopeful

Expanded definition: _____

_____

Additional texts: _____

Enduring

Expanded definition: _____

_____

_____

Additional texts: _____

_____

Living Insights

Definitions and cross-references are important, but more critical is the whole realm of *application*. Let's do some thinking on how these aspects of love manifest themselves in our lives.

- Using our list from Study One, write down the traits in which you are strong and those you could use some help with. Then develop a strategy to improve some of your weaker areas.

Love in My Life

My personal strengths: _____

_____

_____

My personal weaknesses: _____

_____

_____

My strategy for improving my practice of love: _____

_____

_____

_____

_____

_____

What about Tongues in the Church Today?

1 Corinthians 14:1–25

Two congregations of differing denominations were located only a few blocks from each other in a small community. They thought it might be better if they would merge and become one united body, larger and more effective, rather than two struggling churches. Good idea ... but both were too petty to pull it off. The problem? They couldn't agree on how they would recite the Lord's Prayer. One group wanted "forgive us our trespasses" while the other demanded "forgive us our debts." So the newspaper reported that one church went back to its trespasses while the other returned to its debts![1]

As silly as this story seems, it's a classic case of majoring on the minors. Ever since the apostles formed the first church, doctrinal nit-picking has caused discord and conflict within and between congregations. Pre-Tribulation Rapture or post? Permanent salvation or temporary? Should women preach? Should priests marry? And then there's the topic of tongues.

Sincerely seeking the truth, Christians today are asking questions like, How important is this gift? Should we strive to speak in tongues? Does the gift of tongues belong in our churches? Is it really a spiritual gift, or simply an ecstatic emotional high?

Curious and confused, the church at Corinth plied Paul with similar questions almost two thousand years ago. In this lesson, we will study the response he gave in 1 Corinthians 14:1–25, where he provided strict guidelines on the value and role of tongues. As we examine his answers, we'll gain insight into handling this issue in our own churches. Basing our study solely on Scripture, and not on experience, let's allow God's Word to speak for itself.

I. Four Introductory Remarks

Before we get into the structure of this passage, let's survey our foundation.

A. We are studying 1 Corinthians, not tongues. It's easy to come upon a topic like this and get sidetracked by the pros and cons or bogged down in details. We could easily devote an

---

1. Charles R. Swindoll, *Growing Strong in the Seasons of Life* (Portland, Oreg.: Multnomah Press, 1983), p. 286.

entire study guide to tongues, but for now, we're working our way through 1 Corinthians, not through a topical study.[2]

B. The main subject of chapters 12–14 is spiritual gifts as a whole, not just speaking in tongues. The gift of tongues is emphasized in chapter 14, but only as it relates to all the spiritual gifts and to the entire body of believers.

C. Paul addresses chapter 14 to a local church, not an individual. Because speaking in tongues is a spiritual gift, and spiritual gifts should benefit the whole church, Paul is dealing with tongues as a public gift rather than a private experience.

D. Paul wants to correct a problem in the Corinthian church, not elevate the gift of tongues. Paul knew that the Corinthians were abusing this gift. He spends time on this, not to exalt it, but to show its insignificance in relation to other gifts.[3]

II. Tongues and Prophecy

Gently transitioning from his eloquent chapter on love, Paul evaluates the gift of tongues by contrasting it with the gift of prophecy.

Pursue love, yet desire earnestly spiritual gifts, but especially that you may prophesy. (v. 1)

"Pursue love," Paul says. "Chase after it, strive for it. Love should be your ultimate goal. But when it comes to spiritual gifts, prophecy is the one you should desire."

> ### What Is Prophecy?
> We tend to think of prophecy as predicting the future. But before the Scriptures were complete, God's inerrant, inspired message was communicated to the early Church through the lips of recognized prophets.
>
> Prophets had to have "a message from God in the form of special revelation, . . . guidance regarding its declaration so that it would be given forth accurately, and the message itself had to have the authority of God."[4]
>
> The prophet was much needed in the first century because the New Testament Church didn't have the complete Word of

2. If you would like to do further study on the gift of tongues, three good resources are *Tongues: An Answer to Charismatic Confusion,* by Charles R. Swindoll (Portland, Oreg.: Multnomah Press, 1981); *The Modern Tongues Movement,* by Robert G. Gromacki (Phillipsburg, N.J.: Presbyterian and Reformed Publishing Co., 1974); and *The Charismatics,* by John F. MacArthur, Jr. (Grand Rapids, Mich.: Zondervan Publishing House, 1978).

3. The Bible lists spiritual gifts in only four passages (Rom. 12, 1 Cor. 12, Eph. 4, and 1 Pet. 4). The gift of tongues is mentioned only in 1 Corinthians 12 and is placed last or next to last each time. Note the order of priority in 1 Corinthians 12:28.

4. John F. Walvoord, "Spiritual Gifts Today," *Bibliotheca Sacra* (October–December 1973), p. 319.

> God bound in their own tongue as we do today. So the prophet
> came and ministered the Word until the Word came to minister
> prophecy.

A. Prophecy is superior for the insider. In verses 1–19,
Paul addresses the insiders—believers who belonged to the
church. After declaring the superiority of prophecy to tongues
in verse 1, Paul gives three reasons that back up his claim.

1. Tongues don't edify the church, but prophecy does
(vv. 2–4). Paul illustrates this idea in verses 2–3.

> For one who speaks in a tongue does not speak
> to men, but to God; for no one understands, but
> in his spirit he speaks mysteries. But one who
> prophesies speaks to men for edification and
> exhortation and consolation.

Derived from the Greek word *oikodomē, edification* means
"to be built up." It involves strengthening with knowledge
on the inside and convicting with information on the outside. According to verse 4, only the speaker is edified when
tongues are spoken. But when prophecy is relayed, both
speaker and hearer benefit—the whole church is built up,
strengthened, and encouraged (compare vv. 12, 17, 26).

**2. Tongues don't benefit the hearer without an interpreter,
but prophecy benefits everyone** (vv. 5–15). Paul continues
to emphasize prophecy in verse 5.

> Now I wish that you all spoke in tongues, but
> *even more* that you would prophesy; and greater
> is one who prophesies than one who speaks in
> tongues, *unless he interprets,* so that the church
> may receive edifying. (emphasis added)

Again Paul stresses edification. And tongues must be interpreted for the church body to benefit from them. To illustrate the importance of interpretation, Paul uses three
analogies: musical instruments, the battle cry of the bugle,
and language itself (vv. 7–9). If notes played on the flute
and harp are not distinguished by tone, pitch, and time,
they are only noises, not music. If the buglar just blows
random notes, how can the troops know whether to march
or retreat? And language must be clear and distinct for the
message to be understood.

> If then I do not know the meaning of the lan-
> guage, I shall be to the one who speaks a barbar-
> ian, and the one who speaks will be a barbarian to

me.[5] . . . Therefore let one who speaks in a tongue
pray that he may interpret. (vv. 11, 13)

3. Tongues don't instruct the assembly, but prophecy does
(vv. 16–19). Paul makes a third point in favor of prophecy.
Otherwise if you bless in the spirit only, how will
the one who fills the place of the ungifted say
the "Amen" at your giving of thanks, since he
does not know what you are saying? For you are
giving thanks well enough, but the other man is
not edified. I thank God, I speak in tongues more
than you all; however, in the church I desire to
speak five words with my mind, that I may instruct others also, rather than ten thousand words
in a tongue.
Paul readily admits that he speaks in tongues, but he's reluctant to do so in public. To him, five words with meaning
and clarity are more important than ten thousand words in
a language that doesn't enlighten those around him.

B. Prophecy is also superior for the outsider (vv. 20–25).
Not only is prophecy a better teaching tool for believers, it is
more helpful for unbelievers and church visitors too. In this final
passage of our study, Paul explains the original purpose of
tongues and the response others have toward this gift.

1. Purpose of the gift of tongues (vv. 20–22). Paul begins
verse 20 by exhorting the Corinthians to be mature, to grow
up in their thinking. He reflects on the words of the prophet
Isaiah (Isa. 28:11–12), who warned unbelieving Israel that
God's judgment was approaching. How were they to know
this? Through the foreign tongues of Assyria's army.[6] Based
on Isaiah's declaration, Paul concludes that "tongues are for
a sign . . . to unbelievers" (1 Cor. 14:22a). Prophecy, however,
is a sign to believers (v. 22b). While the gift of tongues
reaches the lost, prophecy teaches the saved.

2. Response to the gift of tongues (vv. 23–25). Paul realizes
that a negative response to tongues could determine a negative response to Christ and His Church, so he tenaciously
continues to reason with the Corinthians:
If therefore the whole church should assemble
together and all speak in tongues, and ungifted

---

5. To the Greek, a barbarian was anyone who did not speak Greek.

6. This fits perfectly with the Pentecost account in Acts 2:1–11, where the foreign languages
uttered by the apostles were a sign to some of Jerusalem's unbelieving Jews. God used tongues
to get their attention, and they heard the gospel in their language for the first time.

men or unbelievers enter, will they not say that you are mad? (v. 23)

But Paul said in verse 22 that tongues are for the unbeliever. What does he mean now? Apparently, the Corinthians were not speaking the languages of those in the assembly, and there were no interpreters. Imagine the scene: someone stands up and speaks unintelligible words, followed by another, and another. No interpretation is given, and the unbeliever or visitor leaves the Corinthian church in confusion, concluding that the people are crazy. The Greek term Paul uses for *mad* means "mania"—mania pervaded the place.

But if all prophesy, and an unbeliever or an ungifted man enters, he is convicted by all, he is called to account by all; the secrets of his heart are disclosed; and so he will fall on his face and worship God, declaring that God is certainly among you. (vv. 24–25)

Prophecy not only instructs believers but also convicts unbelievers because they can understand it—it's in their own language. This understanding begins a process involving conviction, disclosure, worship, and finally acknowledgment of God's presence; and it applies equally to today's unbeliever who hears the preaching of God's Word.

III. Tongues Today

Before we conclude our study, let's discuss two final questions that may be lingering in the back of your mind.

A. Is the gift of tongues available today? Back in Paul's day, the New Testament had not been completed, so the Jews and Gentiles received and confirmed God's Word through tongues and prophecy. But once the Scriptures were complete, these gifts were no longer needed (compare 13:8–10). A former charismatic pastor wrestled with this question and came to the following conclusion.

The inescapable dilemma is this: if the mystery of Christ has been fully revealed, then prophetic revelations can add nothing to it. If, however, tongues and prophecy are confined to the boundaries of canonical Scripture (as many assert), then they are not, properly speaking, revelations—they are repetitions and as such are superfluous. Furthermore, since these gifts functioned to confirm the giving of new revelation, then their purpose has been entirely fulfilled.[7]

7. Neil Babcox, *A Search for Charismatic Reality* (Portland, Oreg.: Multnomah Press, 1985), p. 69.

B. What if I feel I do have the gift of tongues? If you feel you have the gift of tongues, we suggest you test the authenticity of your experience. Tape record yourself while speaking in that tongue and then find three or four people who claim to have the gift of interpretation. If their separate interpretations are identical and don't conflict with Scripture, perhaps you do have this gift. Examine your heart and the Scriptures. Let God's Word be your guide.

> **The Real Issue**
>
> It's not important that we all agree on tongues. Of far more importance is your position with Christ. Have you embraced Him as Lord and Savior? Have you received the greatest gift of all—His love? That's the real issue. Without love, though you speak with the tongues of men and angels, you'll come across like a noisy gong or a clanging cymbal.

 Living Insights

Study One

What about tongues in the Church today? For many, this question is one that requires serious study. It cannot be answered flippantly. This lesson and the next one give us ample opportunity to begin a detailed study of this issue.

- One of the most valuable assets a Bible student can possess is the ability to ask questions. Questions encourage observation, and observation helps develop interpretation. So, as you read through the first twenty-five verses of 1 Corinthians 14, jot down your questions in the chart below; then search for the answers right there in the text.

1 Corinthians 14:1–25		
Verses	Questions	Answers

Continued on next page

29

Verses	Questions	Answers

🗿 *Living Insights*

Study Two ▬▬▬▬▬▬▬▬▬▬▬▬▬▬▬▬▬▬▬▬▬▬▬▬▬▬

If you are involved in a church, it has probably taken a position on speaking in tongues. But what do *you* believe about speaking in tongues? Have you come up with your own position, based on your own study?

• Using the space provided, describe your thoughts on this issue. Remember, base your conclusions on your understanding of the Scriptures, not on what your church, pastor, or teacher says.

My Understanding of Tongues in the Church Today

_____

_____

_____

_____

_____

_____

_____

_____

_____

_____

_____

_____

An Answer to Confusion about Tongues
1 Corinthians 14:26–40

Personal opinion based on experience offers shaky, often erroneous evidence, no matter how sincerely we believe in it. John Godfrey Sacks wrote a story titled "The Blind Men and the Elephant" that illustrates this truth.

In this tale, six blind men from Industan wanted to know the truth about elephants, so they gathered their own facts by going straight to the source.

The first blind man fell against the animal's sturdy side and decided, "The elephant is very like a wall."

The second, feeling the elephant's smooth, sharp tusk, exclaimed, "This wonder of an elephant is very like a spear."

When the third blind man approached the animal, he grabbed its squirming trunk in his hands and promptly declared, "The elephant is very like a snake."

The fourth felt the elephant's rough-skinned leg and determined that it clearly "is very like a tree."

The fifth, having touched its ear, exclaimed that "this marvel of an elephant is very like a fan."

When the sixth blind man groped for what he could call "elephant," the animal's swinging tail fell into his hands, so he explained, "The elephant is very like a rope."

And so these men of Industan disputed loud and long,
Each in his own opinion exceeding stiff and strong,
Though each was partly in the right and all were in the wrong.[1]

If you wanted to discover the real definition of an elephant, you wouldn't ask the six blind men from Industan. Instead, you would go to an encyclopedia and study an article written by experts on elephants. So, too, we need not base the truth about spiritual issues on man's subjective, shortsighted experience.

Unfortunately, many fail to base their opinions on Scripture—the only objective source of truth. In our discussion of 1 Corinthians 14:26–40,

---

1. John Godfrey Sacks, "The Blind Men and the Elephant," as quoted by Charles R. Swindoll in *Tongues: An Answer to Charismatic Confusion* (Portland, Oreg.: Multnomah Press, 1981), pp. 3–4.

however, we will set all human experience aside and gather our guidelines solely from God's Word.

I. The Edification Principle

The first gate the experience of tongues must pass through is the gate of results.

> What is the outcome then, brethren? When you assemble, each one has a psalm, has a teaching, has a revelation, has a tongue, has an interpretation. Let all things be done for edification. (v. 26)

Paul's comment tells us something of the way the early Church worshiped.

> The really notable thing about an early Church service must have been that almost everyone came feeling that he had both the privilege and the obligation of contributing something to it. A man did not come with the sole intention of being a passive listener; he came not only to receive but to give.[2]

In the first-century Church, worship was a spontaneous experience. They didn't have a completed Bible, so they waited upon God to finalize truth through the gifts of the Body's members. As the Spirit swept through the Church, all were confident that whatever was spoken, sung, or taught was directly from God—for the purpose of edifying, building up the Body.

Does It Build Up?

When hearing others speak in tongues, are you spiritually strengthened, encouraged to love and serve God more faithfully and devoutly? If not, the biblical truth about tongues is not being practiced.

II. The Procedure Principle

Another guideline for determining the biblical use of tongues is found in verse 27a.

> If anyone speaks in a tongue, it should be by two or at the most three, and each in turn.

When simultaneous utterances are made, confusion results. So, Paul explains that tongues should never be spoken by more than three people during a worship service and never by more than one person at a time. Many would argue, Why must we be so literal? If the Spirit prompts more than one person to speak at a time, who are we to

---

2. William Barclay, *The Letters to the Corinthians,* rev. ed., The Daily Study Bible Series (Philadelphia, Pa.: Westminster Press, 1975), pp. 134–35.

keep this overflow of power tight under a lid? Yet it's interesting that we have no trouble taking literally the other procedures laid out in the Bible—such procedures as communion (1 Cor. 11:17–34) and confronting a brother or sister in sin (Matt. 18:15–17). Paul has set down a literal procedure for the gift of tongues, and any violation of that is a violation of truth.

III. The Interpretation Principle

Walking hand in hand with the procedure principle is the principle of interpretation.

> And let one interpret; but if there is no interpreter, let him keep silent in the church; and let him speak to himself and to God. (1 Cor. 14:27b–28)

A genuine message spoken in tongues was always to be followed by an interpretation so that the whole body could be edified. In Corinth, the popularity of speaking in tongues had spread like wildfire, so Paul contains its flame by allowing tongues to be used only when accompanied by the gift of interpretation. If prophecy, which is spoken in the common language, were to be judged by others (see v. 29), how much more does this gift require validation? Paul further contrasts tongues with prophecy to show that tongues should never produce confusion.

> But if a revelation is made to another who is seated, let the first keep silent. For you can all prophesy one by one, so that all may learn and all may be exhorted; and the spirits of prophets are subject to prophets; for God is not a God of confusion but of peace, as in all the churches of the saints. (vv. 30–33)

Contrary to the beliefs of some, any gift the Spirit gives, He can control.

Loving Control

David Prior explains the often overlooked truth about the gift of tongues.

Speaking in tongues ... is not an uncontrollable phenomenon. The person with the gift can choose either to use it or not to use it ... in private or in public.... For this reason it is very misleading to use such language as 'ecstasy' ... to describe any of the Spirit's gifts, but particularly speaking in tongues. Such terminology re-introduces pagan concepts and experiences into the arena of God's operations. His Spirit does not override the wills and minds of human beings. On the contrary, in his

---

love he wins our willing co-operation, and he never forces us to do anything.[3]

IV. The Silence-Subjection Principle

In verses 34–35, Paul gives another guideline to regulate the use of tongues, and in doing so, he raises a question that transcends the subject of gifts altogether.

> Let the women keep silent in the churches; for they are not permitted to speak, but let them subject themselves, just as the Law also says. And if they desire to learn anything, let them ask their own husbands at home; for it is improper for a woman to speak in church.

The word *speak* in this passage refers to more than just tongues. It includes any kind of communication given in an authoritative position.[4] Although created equal (see Gal. 3:28), women have been placed in subjection to men (1 Tim. 2:12). They therefore have no right to assume a role of authority—whether it's a message of teaching from behind the pulpit or a message in tongues from the pew.

A Signpost

Do you know of any churches whose leadership is dominated by women?

Clearly, churches with female leadership cut across the grain of Scripture—a sure sign that they are not taking the principles of Scripture to heart.

V. The Dignity Principle

The Corinthian believers saw themselves as pacesetters, originators of truth, the first to receive God's instructions. Paul responds to their elitist spirit with a sarcastic bite.

> Was it from you that the word of God first went forth? Or has it come to you only? If anyone thinks he is a prophet or spiritual, let him recognize that the things which I write to you are the Lord's commandment. (1 Cor. 14:36–37)

---

3. David Prior, *The Message of 1 Corinthians: Life in the Local Church* (Downers Grove, Ill.: InterVarsity Press, 1985), pp. 250–51.

4. We know this because the word Paul uses here for *speak* is *laleō*—the most familiar Greek word for speaking, used in this chapter twenty-four times, often with reference to common, everyday talk (see v. 19).

What audacity the Corinthians had to assume that it all started in Corinth! Yet these conceited believers weren't even following God's instructions. As Paul told them, if they ignored the fact that his teaching was from the Lord, they, in turn, would be ignored (v. 38). After giving this warning, Paul distills his instructions into one final principle:

Therefore, my brethren, desire earnestly to prophesy, and do not forbid to speak in tongues. But let all things be done properly and in an orderly manner. (vv. 39–40)

A worship service ought to be a beautiful, meaningful experience. It should be warm and have a spontaneity that the Spirit is delighted to prompt. All of this, without a trace of confusion.

Seeing Eyes

Some church services throw dignity to the wind. They give little thought to the proper, biblical way of worshiping and base the right and wrong of it all on their own experience.

William Barclay contrasts this attitude with the way things should be done:

There must be liberty but there must be no disorder. The God of peace must be worshipped in peace.[5]

In forming our opinions on the issues raised by the charismatic movement, let's not mimic the blind men of Industan. Instead, let's turn to the Bible—the encyclopedia of truth—and let its teaching validate our experience.

 Living Insights

Study One ■━━━━━━━━━━━━━━━━━━━━━━━━━━━━━━

This is an extremely important passage of Scripture, one not easily taken in at the first reading. Perhaps it would be helpful to take a step back and approach this text in a fresh way.

● Read 1 Corinthians 14 from a different version of the Bible. Sometimes seeing the familiar text in a different light will let you discover new shades of meaning and understanding. Read slowly and carefully.

Continued on next page

---

5. Barclay, *Letters to the Corinthians,* p. 134.

Living Insights

Some people are fighters. Few things hurt the cause of Christ more! The last verse of this chapter emphasizes dignity, beauty, harmony, humility, unity, and order. What are you doing to promote that sort of goodwill among the members of the Body of Christ?

• Instead of loading your shotgun with newfound material concerning tongues, turn your attention to the promotion of harmony and order. Use the space provided to jot down some specific things you can do this week to promote unity and love among believers. If you *really* want to show love and harmony, do something special this week for someone with whom you disagree.

How I'll Show Love and Harmony This Week

_____

_____

_____

_____

_____

_____

_____

_____

_____

_____

_____

_____

_____

_____

Back from the Dead!

1 Corinthians 15:1–11

Most people find some part of the gospel message a bitter pill to swallow, a part at which they sneer their rejections, ever keeping the good news at arm's length.

The ancient Greeks were no exception. Because of their pride in their advanced intellects, they found it difficult to embrace the Resurrection of Christ.

In Athens' citadel of human philosophy, the Areopagus, believing in the resurrection of the body was unthinkable. The Greeks believed the body to be the source of man's weakness and sin; they viewed it as a corpse, a tomb. Therefore, they looked upon death with joy, anxiously awaiting the time when their souls would be liberated, unshackled from their bodies.

Located near Athens, Corinth was greatly influenced by this Greek mindset. Being a city that valued pleasure above learning, Corinth left the thinking to her Athenian neighbors, adopting their attitudes toward the resurrection of the body without question.

Although the Christians at Corinth had accepted the Resurrection of the Lord, they still denied the resurrection of their own bodies (1 Cor. 15:12). So, in 1 Corinthians 15, Paul builds his case for the resurrection of the body with a simple, yet persuasive, argument: Because Christ has risen from the dead and promised that believers will also be raised, we must either accept our resurrection or reject Christ's. And since the Resurrection of Christ is a historical fact, we must believe in it and the resurrection of our bodies as well.

Paul spends the first eleven verses of this chapter building the foundation for his argument—validating the Lord's Resurrection.

I. The Gospel of Christ

The heartbeat of resurrection theology is the gospel. So, in verses 1–4, this is where Paul begins.

A. The process. Every time the gospel is presented and accepted it goes through the same process.

> Now I make known to you, brethren, the gospel which
> I preached to you, which also you received, in which
> also you stand. (v. 1)

There's always a vehicle of knowledge—whether a person, the Bible, or other literature—always a recipient, and always the same result, someone standing for the first time on the solid rock of God's truth. This process isn't restricted to the pulpit. In fact, pulpit preaching often constricts the heart of a sinner.

Informally sharing the gospel can reach people that preaching never could. It doesn't need a pulpit. It can be done across the kitchen table, over the back fence, from one desk to another—wherever. All it takes for salvation to be secured is a willing vehicle, a ready recipient, and a right response to the truth.

B. The objective. Salvation from sin isn't God's only goal for us. He's also concerned that we be saved from ourselves—the stubborn, strong, sinewy self-will that constantly entangles our new selves (see Rom. 7). We see that Paul has this second objective in mind through his choice of words in verse 2:

> By which also you *are* saved, if you hold fast the
> word which I preached to you, unless you believed
> in vain. (emphasis added)

Notice that he doesn't say "were saved," which would indicate the one-time, ever-secure acceptance of salvation. But he says "are saved," which means that this kind of salvation is an ongoing process. Also, the "word" Paul preached to them is an allusion to the daily denying of self, taking up your cross and following the Lord (see Luke 9:23). Paul is saying that if our belief is only surface, if no signs of victory over sin are growing from the soil of our lives, we have believed in vain.

Going below the Surface

In *Mere Christianity,* C. S. Lewis comments on the difficulty we have in letting the Lord get beneath the surface to change us.

The terrible thing, the almost impossible thing, is to hand over your whole self—all your wishes and precautions—to Christ. But it is far easier than what we are all trying to do instead. For what we are trying to do is to remain what we call "ourselves," to keep personal happiness as our great aim in life, and yet at the same time be "good." We are all trying to let our mind and heart go their own way—centred on money or pleasure or ambition—and hoping, in spite of this, to behave honestly and chastely and humbly. And that is exactly what Christ warned us you could not do. As He said, a thistle cannot produce figs. If I am a field that contains nothing but grass-seed, I cannot produce wheat. Cutting the grass may keep it short: but I shall still produce grass and no wheat. If I want to

---

> produce wheat, the change must go deeper than
> the surface. I must be ploughed up and re-sown.[1]

C. The content. Beginning in verse 3, Paul lays out the two main tenets of the gospel.

   1. Christ died. Paul writes, "For I delivered to you as of first importance what I also received, that Christ died for our sins according to the Scriptures, and that He was buried" (vv. 3–4a). The sin Christ died for was our selfish independence, our rejection of His way—the way of righteousness. As Isaiah wrote,

   > But He was pierced through for our transgressions,
   > He was crushed for our iniquities;
   > The chastening for our well-being fell upon Him,
   > And by His scourging we are healed.
   > All of us like sheep have gone astray,
   > Each of us has turned to his own way;
   > But the Lord has caused the iniquity of us all
   > To fall on Him. (Isa. 53:5–6)

   Jesus' burial is proof of His death. Those who loved Him . . . who took His body, embalmed it, and wrapped it carefully in grave clothes saw no sign of life, or they surely wouldn't have buried Him.

   2. Christ rose. In verse 4b, Paul nutshells the gospel message:

   > He was raised on the third day according to the
   > Scriptures.

   Believing in the gospel means having faith in the fact that Jesus Christ not only died for you but was also raised for you. It means coming to the cross empty-handed, clinging only to the crucified Christ and the empty tomb.

II. The Appearances of Christ

After His Resurrection the Lord appeared to people on many occasions. As Luke wrote,

> To these He . . . presented Himself alive, after His suffer-
> ing, by many convincing proofs, appearing to them over
> a period of forty days, and speaking of the things con-
> cerning the kingdom of God. (Acts 1:3)

   A. To the masses. On that first Easter morning, the Lord began to make His Resurrection known.

   > And that He appeared to Cephas, then to the twelve.
   > After that He appeared to more than five hundred

---

1. C. S. Lewis, *Mere Christianity,* rev. and enl. (New York, N.Y.: Macmillan Publishing Co., 1952), p. 168.

brethren at one time, most of whom remain until
now, but some have fallen asleep; then He appeared
to James, then to all the apostles. (1 Cor. 15:5–7)
Numerous eyewitnesses were testimony to the reality of a risen
Lord!

He's Alive!

Skeptics are still trying to explain away the appear-
ances of the risen Christ, but their theories are repeatedly
refuted. In fact, some of their explanations are more in-
credible than the problems they have with Jesus' actual
Resurrection.

One theory is that Jesus never really died. Laid in His
tomb unconscious, He later revived, somehow managed to
shed His grave clothes and get out of the tomb, then suc-
ceeded in convincing the disciples that He had risen from
the dead. D. F. Strauss, himself a skeptic of the Resurrection, found this theory to be completely ridiculous.

It is impossible that a being who had stolen
half-dead out of the sepulchre, who crept about
weak and ill, wanting medical treatment, who
required bandaging, strengthening and indul-
gence, and who still at last yielded to his suf-
ferings, could have given to his disciples the
impression that he was a Conqueror over death
and the grave, the Prince of Life, an impression
which lay at the bottom of their future ministry.
Such a resuscitation could only have weakened
the impression which he had made upon them
in life and in death, at the most could only have
given it an elegiac voice, but could by no possi-
bility have changed their sorrow into enthusiasm, have elevated their reverence into worship.[2]

The only explanation that fits all the facts is that Jesus
actually died, was buried, and rose from the dead. Halle-
lujah! He's alive!

B. To Paul. In verses 8–11, Paul gets personal, telling us what the
Resurrection meant in his life.

And last of all, as it were to one untimely born, He
appeared to me also. (v. 8)

2. D. F. Strauss, as quoted by William Lane Craig in *The Son Rises: The Historical Evidence for the Resurrection of Jesus* (Chicago, Ill.: Moody Press, 1981), pp. 39–40.

Saved, yes)
Delivered, no !

"Untimely born" refers to one who has been miscarried or aborted. In using this imagery to describe himself, Paul contrasts his background to that of the other apostles—the infants who had been chosen, handpicked, trained, developed at the feet of Jesus. When they were born into apostleship, they were perfect examples of the kind of apostle He wanted to raise. Then came the miscarriage . . . Paul. He had been a vile, hateful persecutor of the Church of Christ (v. 9), yet the Lord appeared to him—an "abortion of a man"—and saved him.

III. Signs of Resurrection Life

From the rest of Paul's testimony, we can glean four signs that prove we have not believed in vain, we are daily dying to our sinful selves, and we are being raised to a life of obedience in Christ (see Rom. 6:1–11).

A. An absence of pride. Paul openly admitted his unworthiness, refused to compete with his peers, and recognized his weaknesses.

> For I am the least of the apostles, who am not fit to
> be called an apostle, because I persecuted the church
> of God. (1 Cor. 15:9)

What about you? Do you have an inflated view of your own significance? How important to you is being right, being heard, being known?

B. A genuine appreciation of grace. Paul attributed everything valuable in his life to God's grace.

> But by the grace of God I am what I am, and His
> grace toward me did not prove vain. (v. 10a)

Does your life echo these words? Do you let grace touch your relationships, home, job, ministry—every part of your life?

C. A humble admission of accomplishments. Paul didn't deny the fact that he had accomplished much for the Lord. His humility was genuine; it allowed him to be honest about his strengths while acknowledging their source. Paul writes:

> But I labored even more than all of them, yet not I,
> but the grace of God with me. (v. 10b)

Do you belittle your accomplishments, parading a false humility before others? Or do you admit what the Lord has enabled you to do through His grace?

D. An honest appreciation of others. Although Paul admitted that he had "labored even more than all of them," he wasn't concerned about who got the credit.

> Whether then it was I or they, so we preach and so
> you believed. (v. 11)

41

If you haven't lost your competitive spirit, if you're always concerned with being number one, ask God to give you a genuine appreciation for others. Only then will you be delivered from your critical, narrow mind-set to a love relationship with the resurrected Lord.

Untimely Born

Like Paul, all of us who believe in Christ have been plucked from our crippled pasts. We may not have persecuted Christ's cause like Paul did, but we all denied His Resurrection in our own subtle ways (Isa. 53:6a).

And just as He did with Paul, so Jesus has brought salvation to us! He has heaped grace upon grace in our lives.

I urge you to embrace the full resurrection message: He has promised not only to give us eternal life but also to give us abundant life—daily—as we soften our hearts, surrender our wills, and obey Him.

 Living Insights

Study One ▬▬▬▬▬▬▬▬▬▬▬▬▬▬▬▬▬▬▬▬▬▬▬▬

Acts 17 is a helpful context for understanding 1 Corinthians 15. The apostle Paul's remarks at the Areopagus set the stage for conveying the importance of Christ's Resurrection. Let's look more closely at his speech.

● Read Acts 17:16–34; then record in the chart below some of your observations regarding Paul's style in reaching this group of philosophers. Ask yourself questions like, What was Paul's purpose in speaking with this group? How did he go about achieving this?

Paul's Address to the Athenians	
Verses	Observations

Living Insights

How can you be sure that you have not believed in vain? Our study ended with four signs to look for; how evident are these four areas in *your* life?

● Take time to reflect on the questions below. Try to answer them honestly, readily admitting areas of weakness but avoiding the pitfall of false modesty.

1. Do I see a marked absence of pride in my life? _____

_____

_____

_____

2. Do I acknowledge and genuinely appreciate God's grace toward me?

_____

_____

_____

3. Can I humbly admit my accomplishments? _____

_____

_____

_____

4. Is an honest appreciation of others characteristic of my life?

_____

_____

_____

What If There Were No Resurrection?

1 Corinthians 15:12–19

Still, black morning.

The phone rings you awake, and before you even realize you've picked it up and said hello, you hear a grief-stricken voice struggling to get the news out:

"He's dead." And your mind races frantically in a frozen fog.

Death.

The Grim Reaper strikes. He honors no hour. Respects no person. Tragic. Unexpected.

Death. Chilling the heart. Leaving a vacuum. Paralyzed, vacant heart. Mind flashing a zillion thoughts—and numb. Hopes dashed. Love lost.

Death.

We've all felt its sting. But for those of us who believe in Christ, there is a balm. A sweet balm. The resurrection.

The resurrection is all we have to cling to when death has stripped a loved one from our arms. It's the solace of a sooncoming spring in the bitter breeze of death's darkest winter. Without it, our lives would have no hope or meaning.

I. If the Resurrection Is False

The Corinthians had rejected the hope of the resurrection. They had bought into the Greek philosophy that the body was the perishable, even contaminated seat of man's sin. Therefore, although they accepted the Lord's Resurrection, they rejected the idea of the resurrection of their own bodies. So in 1 Corinthians 15:12–19, Paul lays the Corinthians' position permanently to rest.

A. If Christ wasn't raised. Denying the resurrection of our bodies requires that we also deny the Lord's Resurrection. As Paul reiterates:

> But if there is no resurrection of the dead, not even Christ has been raised. (v. 13)

How do those who deny Jesus' Resurrection explain the displaced stone? Why were the Roman soldiers guarding His tomb bribed to lie about what happened to His body (Matt. 28:11–15)? Why is His body yet to be found? What about the fact that He appeared to more than five hundred people in His resurrected body (1 Cor. 15:6)? Those who deny the resurrection of our

Vs 21
22

23 - fwd.

1st Fruit offering. Barley sample initial from abundant harvest. ie. in oven cake or rolls in progress.

taste of cooking.

44

bodies must also deny the Lord's Resurrection. And, in the face of these facts, that's a heavy burden of proof to carry.

B. Our preaching is hollow. Like dominoes, Paul's second argument joins the force of the first to topple the Corinthians' reasoning.

> And if Christ has not been raised, then our preaching
> is vain.[1] (v. 14a)

Without the Resurrection, the good news of Christ is no news at all. The gospel message has no validity because it's based on just another good man who lived and died for just another good cause. John Stott puts it well:

> Christianity is Christ. The person and work of Christ
> are the rock upon which the Christian religion is
> built. If he is not who he said he was, and if he did
> not do what he said he had come to do, the founda-
> tion is undermined and the whole superstructure will
> collapse. Take Christ from Christianity, and you dis-
> embowel it; there is practically nothing left. Christ is
> the centre of Christianity; all else is circumference.[2]

C. Our faith is vain. Without the Resurrection, not only is our message in vain, but our faith is useless (v. 14b). As Paul explains in verse 17a:

> And if Christ has not been raised, your faith is worth-
> less.

Without His Resurrection, our faith will never change our lives. Because only the Resurrection gives us power to change.

Resurrection Power—Power to Change

When driving past a huge dam that holds back untold millions of gallons of water, you would probably marvel at all the power harnessed there. But to see the greatest evidence of the dam's power, you would need to travel to a residential area, walk into a darkened room, flip the switch on the wall, and watch the room light up.

In the same way, the power of the Resurrection is best evidenced not in a fantastic display of faith but in the most intimate places of our hearts, where we can see that the darkness has been changed to light.

Are there signs of resurrection power in your life? Are dark corners in your heart being illuminated by the Lord and transformed into areas of holiness?

---

1. Derived from the Greek word *kenos*, *vain* means "empty, or void of content."

2. John R. W. Stott, *Basic Christianity*, 2d ed. (Downers Grove, Ill.: InterVarsity Press, 1971), p. 21.

D. We are liars. In verse 15, Paul knocks the Corinthians' position straight into the grave.

> Moreover we are even found to be false witnesses of God, because we witnessed against God that He raised Christ, whom He did not raise, if in fact the dead are not raised.

If there were no Resurrection, everyone who claimed to have seen the resurrected Lord is a liar. This means Paul . . . Peter . . . the apostles . . . James . . . the five hundred. Also, every Christian thinker and leader who has forged out our faith has lied—Augustine, Aquinas, John Calvin, Martin Luther, John Wesley, Charles Spurgeon, C. S. Lewis. Even Christ Himself—who predicted His own Resurrection and the resurrection of all men (see John 2:18–22, 5:25–29), who convinced people later to be martyred because they believed He had risen from the dead, who is considered the greatest moral teacher of all time—even He was a liar if there is no resurrection.

E. We are lost in our sins. Paul adds another point to his argument in verse 17: "And if Christ has not been raised, . . . you are still in your sins." Yet, as Psalm 103:1–4a tells us, we have been pardoned, healed, and redeemed!

> Bless the Lord, O my soul;
> And all that is within me, bless His holy name.
> Bless the Lord, O my soul,
> And forget none of His benefits;
> Who pardons all your iniquities;
> Who heals all your diseases;
> Who redeems your life from the pit.

If He had remained dead in His tomb, we would still be dead in our sins. His death was only the beginning of healing our sin-diseased hearts. It is His Resurrection that makes us completely whole, completely free from the shackles of sin!

Straight Talk from Paul to You

"Well then, shall we keep on sinning so that God can keep on showing us more and more kindness and forgiveness?

"Of course not! Should we keep on sinning when we don't have to? For sin's power over us was broken when we became Christians and were baptized to become a part of Jesus Christ; through his death the power of your sinful nature was shattered. Your old sin-loving nature was buried with him by baptism when he died, and when God the Father, with glorious power, brought him back to life again, you were given his wonderful new life to enjoy.

"For you have become a part of him, and so you died with him, so to speak, when he died; and now you share his new life, and shall rise as he did. Your old evil desires were nailed to the cross with him; that part of you that loves to sin was crushed and fatally wounded, so that your sin-loving body is no longer under sin's control, no longer needs to be a slave to sin." (Rom. 6:1–6)[3]

F. **Dead believers have perished.** If there is no resurrection, then those also who have fallen asleep in Christ have perished. (v. 18)

Notice the stark contrast between the words "in Christ" and "have perished." Together they're incongruous. Paradoxical. How many times have you, after the death of loved ones, found comfort in the fact that they were with Jesus, where there was no sorrow, no pain, no sickness, no death? Without the resurrection, this hope is mere myth.

G. **We are the most pathetic of all.** The bleak list continues in verse 19:

If we have hoped in Christ in this life only, we are of all men most to be pitied.

Paul's reasoning is captured by David Prior:

If Christ was not raised from the dead, any expectation of life beyond death with him evaporates. We are then left with a pseudo-gospel which purports at least to give some meaning to our life here on earth. This presumably takes the form of doing the best we can to follow the example of Jesus Christ, assuming that we select him as our mentor in preference to countless other teachers, wise men and leaders. Paul sees this attitude to Jesus as pitiable and pathetic: if there is no such thing as resurrection, much of Jesus' teaching falls to the ground and he is revealed to be a liar. Yet the Corinthian Christians had set their hope on Christ as Lord of life, death and eternity. If he was not raised from the dead, he is not Lord of anything. If life here on this earth is all there is, it makes no sense to base our hope on the groundless promises of one who made empty assertions about eternity. If the Christian faith is thus based on an empty gospel

3. The Living Bible (Wheaton, Ill.: Tyndale House Publishers, 1971).

and a fraudulent saviour, 'anybody is better off than the Christian'.[4]

II. Because the Resurrection Is True

But the Resurrection is true! And the gospel is indeed full of power to change our hearts. Because of the resurrection, we are able to hold what we love loosely... we understand that this life isn't all there is. Are you clinging to the gifts, or the giver? Is there something or someone you need to release to the Father's hand? I urge you to let go. Rest in the fact that because He lives, He can give you power to surrender every part of your heart to Him.

 Living Insights

Study One

What if there were no Resurrection? Our study is just starting to reveal what our loss would be if Christ had not risen from the grave. However, before we think through the ramifications of this, it may be helpful to study the historical accounts of Christ's Resurrection.

- Each of the four Gospels gives an account of Christ's Resurrection: Matthew 28:1–17, Mark 16:1–14, Luke 24:1–12, and John 20:1–18. As you read them, use the space provided to summarize the four accounts into one.

Summarizing the Resurrection

asleep — 1st fruits   Dead Christian
Dead Saint — Body only.
Soul is absent from body.
See. ____
Body goes to grave.
"Lost man never said to be asleep."

4. David Prior, *The Message of 1 Corinthians: Life in the Local Church* (Downers Grove, Ill.: InterVarsity Press, 1985), p. 265.

_____

_____

_____

_____

_____

_____

_____

_____

_____

_____

_____

_____

 Living Insights

Study Two ━━━━━━━━━━━━━━━━━━━━━━━━━━━━━

The very foundation of our Christian faith rests on the Resurrection of Jesus Christ. First Corinthians 15 is unmistakable in that regard. But what does the Resurrection mean to you and me personally? Let's consider ways to apply this doctrine to our lives.

• Use the following questions to spark your thoughts regarding ways you can apply the Resurrection to your life.

—How does Christ's Resurrection affect your struggle with sin?
—Does His Resurrection change your view of death?
—Do you see any evidence of Resurrection power in your life?
—How does the Resurrection affect what you value?
—Does the Resurrection give you hope in the dark times of life?

Christ's Unfinished Work
1 Corinthians 15:20–28

Scripture is alive with examples of how to live and how not to live, examples that have broken past the Bible's bound pages and become metaphors in our twentieth-century vocabulary—doubting Thomas, Mary and Martha, a Judas kiss.

One of the most familiar metaphors taken from the Bible is pharisee, picturing a legalistic hypocrite with a heart hot toward the law but numb-cold toward love. And another first-century religious sect—the Sadducees—provides us with a metaphor that fits the modern-day attitudes of many.

The Sadducees didn't care about living up to any conservative tradition. They were the aristocrats, the wealthy—liberals in their theology and rationalists in their philosophy. Anything they couldn't put in a test tube they rejected—the existence of angels, Satan, the resurrection. Adopting reason as their god, they orphaned everything that required faith.[1]

Apparently, some of the believers at Corinth had bought into the Sadducee philosophy. Although they consented to the Lord's Resurrection, they denied the resurrection of their own bodies. To them, it didn't make sense. And since it didn't make sense, they threw it out.

I. Looking Back: Christ's Resurrection

In 1 Corinthians 15:12–19, Paul gave the tragic answer to the question: What if there were no resurrection? Then, beginning with verse 20, he does an about-face. He turns from the hypothetical to the factual, arguing for our resurrection on the basis of Christ's.

A. The fact. Paul states the fact of Christ's Resurrection in verse 20.

But now Christ has been raised from the dead, the first fruits of those who are asleep.

"Those who are asleep" is Paul's euphemism for believers who have died. It's not our souls that sleep—once we die, our souls are present with God (2 Cor. 5:8). But it's our bodies that are peacefully awaiting resurrection. The down payment on our resurrection is the Resurrection of Christ. He is the firstfruits of the abundant harvest yet to come. William Barclay explains the background of this image.

The law[2] laid it down that some sheaves of barley must be reaped from a common field.... When the

---

1. In Matthew 22:23–33, the Sadducees try to pin Jesus with their argument against the resurrection. Instead of answering their peripheral questions, He goes to the heart of the problem with an argument so strong that when He had finished, "they were astonished at His teaching" (v. 33b).

2. See Leviticus 23:10–11.

barley was cut it was brought to the Temple. There it was threshed with soft canes so as not to bruise it. It was then parched over the fire in a perforated pan so that every grain was touched by the fire. It was then exposed to the wind so that the chaff was blown away. It was then ground in a barley mill, and the flour of it was offered to God. That was the first-fruits. And it is very significant to note that not until after that was done could the new barley be bought and sold in the shops and bread be made from the new flour. The first-fruits were a sign of the harvest to come; and the Resurrection of Jesus was a sign of the resurrection of all believers which was to come. Just as the new barley could not be used until the first-fruits had been duly offered, so the new harvest of life could not come until Jesus had been raised from the dead.[3]

B. The result. The outcome of Jesus' Resurrection is described in verses 21–22.

> For since by a man came death, by a man also came the resurrection of the dead. For as in Adam all die, so also in Christ all shall be made alive. (see also Rom. 5:12)

Wherever the Scriptures speak about sin, they also speak about death. The two are inseparable. Whoever experiences one will experience the other. Or, in the Lord's case, whoever triumphs over one, triumphs over the other. Adam brought sin and death into the world, but Christ brought resurrection and life. Like a Jew who took the firstfruits to the temple, Jesus was resurrected and presented to the Father as a sign of the harvest to come— the resurrection of the saints.

Part of the Harvest

Whether we're in Adam or in Christ, we all have eternal life. The difference lies in our destinies.

Those with skeptical, Sadducee-hearts are branches on *Adam's* family tree, which will spend eternity in the lake of fire (see Rev. 20:14). They *can't win.*

But all of us who have accepted *Christ* are part of the living harvest, waiting for Him to gather us up to the Father's presence. For us, there's nothing but *victory* (2 Tim. 2:10–12a).

---

3. William Barclay, *The Letters to the Corinthians,* 2d ed., The Daily Study Bible Series (Philadelphia, Pa.: Westminster Press, 1956), pp. 167–68.

II. Looking Ahead: Our Resurrection

Beginning with verse 23, the emphasis shifts from the past to the future—from Christ's Resurrection to ours. Paul explains our resurrection in relation to some upcoming events. His desire is not to give us a panorama of prophecy but to focus in on a few significant events ahead of us.

A. The order. Without giving a specific time frame, Paul flashes three sequential scenes across the screen of the future.

    1. Christ's coming and the saints' resurrection. The opening scene reveals who will be raised first and who's to follow.

> But each in his own order: Christ the first fruits, after that those who are Christ's at His coming. (v. 23)

    Jesus is the firstborn from the dead (see Col. 1:18, Rev. 1:5), and those who have died believing in Him will be raised next. Firstfruits first, then the harvest. First Thessalonians 4:16–17 describes this miraculous event we know as the Rapture.

> For the Lord Himself will descend from heaven with a shout, with the voice of the archangel, and with the trumpet of God; and the dead in Christ shall rise first. Then we who are alive and remain shall be caught up together with them in the clouds to meet the Lord in the air, and thus we shall always be with the Lord.

    From the time we first meet Jesus face-to-face, we will live with Him forever.

    2. The King's kingdom and His enemies' abolition. Even though the end of Christ's kingdom isn't the next event on our premillennial charts, it's the next scene Paul chooses to show.[4] He continues:

> Then the end will come, when he hands over the kingdom to God the Father after he has destroyed all dominion, authority and power. For he must reign until he has put all his enemies under his feet. The last enemy to be destroyed is death. For he "has put everything under his feet." Now when it says that "everything" has been put under him, it is clear that this does not include God himself, who put everything under Christ. (1 Cor. 15:24–27)[5]

---

4. Between the Rapture and the end of the kingdom, Christ will establish His earthly kingdom and reign for a thousand years (see Rev. 20:4–6).

5. The One Year Bible: The New International Version (Wheaton, Ill.: Tyndale House Publishers, 1986).

During His kingdom reign, Christ will establish Himself as an absolute monarch, the sole authority over all. And when the end comes, He will give the kingdom back to the Father in perfect order. Every enemy will be destroyed—even death. And everything will be in subjection to Him.

3. **The Son's subjection and the Father's acceptance.** Next comes the final scene.

> And when all things are subjected to Him, then
> the Son Himself also will be subjected to the One
> who subjected all things to Him. (v. 28a)

The Lord Jesus was dispatched from heaven to earth knowing He had two missions. The first was to deal with the invisible part of man—his soul—and the invisible enemies, Satan and his host. But His other mission was to deal with the visible—the world, its elements, and man's body. When He died, rose, and ascended, Jesus' words "It is finished" reverberated across heaven because mission one had been accomplished. But He still hasn't completed His second mission. Scripture tells us that our bodies groan for their redemption.

> For we know that the whole creation groans and
> suffers the pains of childbirth together until now.
> And not only this, but also we ourselves, having
> the first fruits of the Spirit, even we ourselves
> groan within ourselves, waiting eagerly for our
> adoption as sons, the redemption of our body.
> (Rom. 8:22–23)

Clearly, redemption is yet to come. After the Lord descends, establishes Himself as the sole authority, and abolishes every enemy, He will go to the Father for the second time and say, "It is finished." And we, for the first time, will experience the fullness of His blessings—and the fullness of our sonship.

> "And He shall wipe away every tear from their
> eyes; and there shall no longer be any death;
> there shall no longer be any mourning, or crying,
> or pain; the first things have passed away. . . . It
> is done. I am the Alpha and the Omega, the be-
> ginning and the end. I will give to the one who
> thirsts from the spring of the water of life without
> cost. He who overcomes shall inherit these things,
> and I will be his God and he will be My son."
> (Rev. 21:4, 6b–7)

B. **The purpose.** All this will be done for one reason: "that God may be all in all" (1 Cor. 15:28b). That He—the triune God—will be recognized by all as sovereign and supreme.

If you accept the clarion call of Christ's Resurrection, rejoice! You, like the Lord Jesus, will be raised to live forever in God's presence.

But if, like the Sadducees, you turn a deaf ear to the good news, you will know only judgment and pain for eternity.

"For a damned soul is nearly nothing: it is shrunk, shut up in itself. Good beats upon the damned incessantly as sound waves beat on the ears of the deaf, but they cannot receive it. Their fists are clenched, their teeth are clenched, their eyes fast shut. First they will not, in the end they cannot, open their hands for gifts, or their mouths for food, or their eyes to see."[6]

Open your eyes and see that the Lord is good! Open your mouth and drink from the spring of the water of life. Open your hands and receive His free gift of salvation. Faith in His Resurrection will secure your soul until His work is finally finished—until we are finally and fully His sons, and He our God (see Rev. 21:7).

 Living Insights

Study One ▬▬▬▬▬▬▬▬▬▬▬▬▬▬▬▬▬▬▬▬▬▬▬▬▬▬▬

Tucked away in the center of 1 Corinthians 15 is an important passage that contrasts mankind *in Adam* and *in Christ*. To further clarify this teaching, let's compare this text to one from the book of Romans.

• Read through 1 Corinthians 15 and Romans 5. Using the following chart, list the differences between life in Adam and life in Christ. After this, if you are in Christ, thank Him for those differences. If you are still in Adam, consider what you've learned in this study, and make the decision to join the *living*. Do that right now, won't you?

---

6. C. S. Lewis, *The Great Divorce* (New York, N.Y.: Macmillan Publishing Co., 1946), p. 123.

The Great Contrast	
In Adam	In Christ

Living Insights

Not only is Christ's Resurrection a glorious fact from the past, it has exciting applications for the future!

- Let's take some time to *pray* about the implications of this lesson. Reflect on His Resurrection and thank Him for all that it means. Then think about your resurrection and praise Him for the bright hope it brings. Make this a time of worship and praise.

If you knew there was no resurrection, no future life. ~~than~~ would you live differently? ie. animals. If no res. Vs. 32 Isah also. If no res. - Eat drink + be merry.

Living for Tomorrow, Today
1 Corinthians 15:29–34

Edgar Allan Poe. One of the most brilliant writers in American history . . . and one of the most misunderstood. His short stories and poems have taken millions of readers deep into the haunting mists of the imagination. Yet, because his peers couldn't see the tragedy in his life, they tagged him insane . . . a hopeless drunk . . . a drug addict. And they failed to honor the truth in his works.

In a masked autobiography, *The Pit and the Pendulum,* Poe draws on his personal despair. He pictures himself strapped into a pit of fate, the razor-sharp blade of death's pendulum swinging above him, moving closer with each swing. No hope, nothing beyond the grave.

Centuries before Poe was born, a man named Job suffered tragedies far greater than Poe ever did. Job felt the sting of sores that covered his entire body. He lost every member of his family, every servant, every possession— and his friends fostered the idea that the God he trusted and served so faithfully had turned on him and stabbed him in the back.

Like Poe, Job expressed his pain in his writings, asking the difficult questions that usually go hand in hand with suffering. In Job 14, we find our protagonist feeling strapped into fate's pit, the pendulum of circum-stances swinging its blade-like reminder of pain and death.

"Man, who is born of woman,
Is short-lived and full of turmoil.
Like a flower he comes forth and withers.
He also flees like a shadow and does not remain." (vv. 1–2)

But, unlike Poe, Job believed in the resurrection.[1] In the midst of his anguish, he spoke these words:

"And as for me, I know that my Redeemer lives,
And at the last He will take His stand on the earth.
Even after my skin is destroyed,
Yet from my flesh I shall see God." (19:25–26)

Every believer of the church at Corinth held to the Resurrection of Christ, but not all of them would have agreed with Job that they, too, would

---

1. Many have interpreted Job 14:14a, "If a man dies, will he live again?" to mean that Job questioned the resurrection of the body after death. But, as one commentator explains, he wasn't inquiring "as to whether a dead man should come back to life; but whether a man dead so far as the physical is concerned, still lives. If a man die, if the flower is cut off, is that man still alive? The question has not to do with a possible return to life, but is concerned with the idea of the continuity of life beyond what men call death." From *The Answers of Jesus to Job* (1935; reprint, Grand Rapids, Mich.: Baker Book House, 1973), p. 43.

be resurrected to see the Lord. So in 1 Corinthians 15:29-34, Paul confronts these Corinthian Poes, arguing for the resurrection from a practical point of view.

I. Questions to Consider

After building his case for resurrection on history (vv. 1–11), theology (vv. 12–19), and prophecy (vv. 20–28), Paul turns to practicality and everyday logic to help carry the burden of proof.

A. If there is no resurrection, why baptize for the dead? With verse 29, Paul opens a can of worms, and theologians today can't seem to agree on how to put a lid on it.

> Otherwise, what will those do who are baptized for the dead? If the dead are not raised at all, why then are they baptized for them?

"Baptized for the dead" probably means being baptized in honor of or out of respect for a dead believer, perhaps a believer who had died a martyr's death or one who had impacted another's life in a special way.[2] Regardless of the interpretation of this verse, Paul's point is clear: If there were no resurrection, if we all died never to see eternity, such a practice would be nothing more than empty liturgy. It would be absurd!

B. If there's no resurrection, why do believers consistently put themselves in danger? In the early Church, being associated with Christianity wasn't one of the more popular things to do. Christians were often persecuted, even killed, for their faith. Paul's logic is plain:

> Why are we also in danger every hour? I protest, brethren, by the boasting in you, which I have in Christ Jesus our Lord, I die daily. . . . If the dead are not raised, let us eat and drink, for tomorrow we die. (vv. 30–31, 32b)

If there's no eternity, why not live it up? Why not say yes to the flesh's cravings? Why die to our desires? Why live to please Christ? If there's no resurrection, we are fools to live pure, holy lives.

C. If there is no resurrection, how can we benefit from living as if there is? The question Paul raises in verse 32 is much like the last one, yet it goes deeper into the matter of motivation and reward. Using startling imagery, Paul writes:

> If from human motives I fought with wild beasts at Ephesus, what does it profit me? (v. 32a)

---

2. For an overview of many of the other interpretations of this verse, see *The Expositor's Bible Commentary*, 12 vols., ed. Frank E. Gaebelein (Grand Rapids, Mich.: Zondervan Publishing House, 1976), vol. 10, pp. 287–88.

Paul's reference to the wild beasts is probably best taken as a metaphor for the adversaries he faced in Ephesus (see 16:8,9).[3] His question is: Why should we put up with the savage attacks of others if there's no life beyond the grave? What is the possible benefit of suffering in this life if there is no hope of heaven?

Now and Then

Paul's questions were originally posed to a cluster of people who didn't believe in the resurrection. But the implications of his questions can sustain our faith as well.

First, belief in the resurrection tightens our ties with believers who have died (15:29). Because of the resurrection, we are connected by a timeless bond to Paul, Peter, the other disciples, our family, friends—any believer who has died.

Second, belief in the resurrection acts as a moral safeguard (v. 32b). Often, the issue at the heart of sensuality isn't moral impurity, but temporal vision. If we kick the door shut toward the idea of a future, it's easy to live guilt-free in impure situations. But remembering that there is a tomorrow, that life isn't just one big "now," will motivate us to live pure lives (3:11–15, 2 Cor. 5:10, Rev. 20:11–15).

Third, belief in the resurrection makes today's trials bearable (1 Cor. 15:32a). Knowing our faith will be rewarded in the future gives us strength to face our own "wild beasts."

We who cling to the hope of the resurrection—is it in theory only? Or are our lives changed? Are we living as if our behavior today will affect our tomorrow?

II. Exhortations to Obey

After arguing from an if-there-were-no-resurrection viewpoint, Paul switches his premise and gives us three commands we need to obey *because there is a resurrection.*

A. Don't be deceived. Quoting a proverb from Greek literature, Paul encourages us to disbelieve those who deny the resurrection.

---

3. The following points all support a metaphorical interpretation of the "wild beasts at Ephesus": (1) as a Roman citizen, Paul probably wouldn't have been thrown into the arena to fight with beasts, since this practice was reserved mainly for those who were heathens, savages, or slaves; (2) in his extensive autobiography in 2 Corinthians 11:22–33, Paul never mentions wild beasts, but instead talks about dangers from his countrymen, "dangers in the city . . . dangers among false brethren" (v. 26); and (3) meticulous Luke, in his record in Acts, doesn't mention wild beasts in relation to Paul. He mentions stoning, trials, ill-treatment, and suffering, but no wild beasts.

Do not be deceived: "Bad company corrupts good morals."⁴ (v. 33)

Here Paul is urging us to listen discerningly. Because if we become enmeshed with ungodly people, their philosophies will become our own. Are you insulated from the world's deceptive philosophies? Do you surround yourself with godly people to imitate?

B. Become sober-minded. In verse 34a, Paul tells us to wake up.

Become sober-minded as you ought.

We've got to be aware of how easy it is to be deceived, to find ourselves whistling the world's tune of "Eat, drink, and be merry, for tomorrow we shall die." We've got to wake up to the fact that our society devours personal identity, encourages mechanistic living and groupthink philosophies. Do you think with discernment? Do you take every thought captive to the obedience of the Lord (see 2 Cor. 10:5b)?

C. Stop sinning. Paul concludes with a catchall command.

And stop sinning; for some have no knowledge of God. I speak this to your shame. (v. 34b)

When the Holy Spirit convicts us of sin, we are to stop, confess it to God, and be cleansed (1 John 1:8–10, 1 Pet. 1:14–16). Nothing is as exciting, satisfying, or rewarding as living a life patterned after godly principles. Nothing!

A Final Thought

Poe's logic wasn't too far wrong. Without the truth of Scripture, we are all strapped into a pit under a pendulum.

But we who can echo Job's words—"I know that my Redeemer lives, . . . even after my skin is destroyed, yet from my flesh I shall see God" (Job 19:25a–26)—need to wake up and stop sinning . . . crawl out of the pit . . . and start living for tomorrow, today.

Continued on next page

---

4. Paul takes this quote, similar in meaning to our "Birds of a feather flock together," from Menander's comedy *Thais.*

Living Insights

In 1 Corinthians 15:29, we are introduced to a fascinating concept: baptism for the dead. This phrase has stimulated quite a bit of discussion within theological circles, but do you know what it means? Let's study this a little further.

- Check some reliable reference materials, such as a Bible dictionary or a commentary. Write down what you learn in the space provided. How does this affect Paul's argument for the resurrection of Christians?

Baptism for the Dead

_____

_____

_____

_____

_____

_____

_____

_____

_____

_____

_____

_____

_____

_____

_____

_____

_____

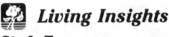 *Living Insights*

Everyone's life tells a story. For some, it's a fairy tale; for others, an adventure novel; for still others, a slow-moving family saga. Have you ever thought of your life as a story? How would you tell it? How have you seen your character develop? What have been the highlights . . . the turning points?

• Try your hand at telling your own story. Use the space that follows to outline your first draft. What has gone into your life that has made you what you are today? Where does the plot seem to be heading? Standing back to get an overview of your life can be an enlightening experience.

My Autobiography

_____

_____

_____

_____

_____

_____

_____

_____

_____

_____

_____

_____

_____

_____

_____

_____

_____

_____

Our Future Bodies
1 Corinthians 15:35–49

When it comes to the resurrection of our bodies, it seems we have more questions than we do answers. Questions that nag. Questions that boggle our minds.

For example, what about babies—will they be resurrected as infants or adults? What happens to the bodies of those who've died violent, tragic deaths—who've been blown up, crushed, dismembered, or lost at sea? And what about people who've been cremated—some whose ashes have been carried away on the wind?

How will God resurrect these people?

Most of our questions stem from a lack of knowledge about the resurrection. Because we can't comprehend the supernatural, we try to cram it into the tiny box of our understanding, which leaves us with a limited view of God, His power, and His ways.

Paul addresses these issues in 1 Corinthians 15:35–49, answering two questions the believers at Corinth had raised. Although his replies don't give us all the specifics, they do give us general principles about our future bodies and a deeper understanding of the value of our present ones.

I. How Can the Dead Possibly Be Raised?
When it came to the teaching that they, like Christ, would be raised, the Corinthians closed the door on their acceptance of the supernatural and, with prideful questions, dared Paul to change their doubting Thomas minds. Their first question is found in verse 35a:

> But someone will say, "How are the dead raised?"

Paul's response is anything but subtle, and he takes the Corinthians back to nature for the answer.

> You fool! That which you sow does not come to life unless it dies. (v. 36)

You can't have a plant unless you have a seed, and seeds are dead. So, every time a seed sprouts life, nature testifies to the fact that life can come from death. In the same way, you can't be resurrected without dying first. Death isn't the enemy of eternal life but its channel. Through death, God gives new life.

Life in Death

Driving through the countryside, you've probably seen fields that have been purposely burned, allowing the soil to replenish itself with the minerals that are its life-giving source. The soil contains only so many minerals, can produce only so many

---

crops before it needs to be scorched, killed—not to become barren, but to prepare for healthy, vibrant life.

What about the soil of your life? Has it yielded too many malnourished crops? Does it need to be purged by the Spirit's fire so it can bear fruit? Trust Him to do this, because He is utterly and wholeheartedly committed to your good (Rom. 8:28).

II. With What Kind of Body Will the Dead Be Raised?

The Corinthians' second question deals with the nature of our resurrected bodies. Paul writes,

> But someone will say, "... And with what kind of body do they come?" (1 Cor. 15:35)

Using analogies and contrasts, Paul invites us to peek behind the curtain of the future.

A. The analogies. Paul paints three word pictures that illustrate what our future bodies will be like.

1. **Seeds.** His first analogy illustrates the continuity of life.

   > And that which you sow, you do not sow the body which is to be, but a bare grain, perhaps of wheat or of something else. (v. 37)

   Although totally different from what it produces, a seed represents the life it will grow. When you plant wheat, you get wheat, not watermelons. When you plant an orange tree, you get oranges, not mangoes. There is a continuity of life shared between the seed and its fruit. And, likewise, our heavenly bodies will be continuations of the life God seeded in the earth's soil. Warren Wiersbe explains:

   > *Resurrection is not reconstruction.* Nowhere does the Bible teach that, at the resurrection, God will "put together the pieces" and return to us our former bodies. There is *continuity* (it is *our* body), but there is not *identity* (it is not the *same* body).[1]

2. **Flesh.** Next Paul talks about the distinctiveness of our future bodies. *Blows halo in evolute*

   > All flesh is not the same flesh, but there is one *in evolute* flesh of men, and another flesh of beasts, and another flesh of birds, and another of fish. (v. 39)

   In creation, God has carefully marked each species with distinctions all its own. And we, too, will continue to bear some of the marks of our present bodies, at least for the purpose of identity. As Jesus' disciples were able to recognize Him in

what about reincarnation

1. Warren W. Wiersbe, *Be Wise* (Wheaton, Ill.: Victor Books, 1983), p. 156.

Beef - fish - birds - human   *Not tossed Salad*

His resurrected body (John 20:19–20), so we will be recognizable and able to identify our loved ones.

3. **Planets.** In his last analogy, Paul pictures the diversity of our future bodies.

> There are also heavenly bodies and earthly bodies, but the glory of the heavenly is one, and the glory of the earthly is another. There is one glory of the sun, and another glory of the moon, and another glory of the stars; for star differs from star in glory. (1 Cor. 15:40–41)

Our future bodies will be different, not only from our present ones, but from those of others. In the same way that no two stars shine with the same brightness, each of us will have a light . . . a glory . . . a purpose all our own.

B. The contrasts. Paul now adds color to his sketch of our resurrected bodies by making a series of contrasts. The following chart will help us see them more clearly.

Earthly Body	Heavenly Body
Perishable	Imperishable
Dishonorable	Glorious
Weak	Powerful
Natural	Spiritual

1. **Perishable versus imperishable.** On all of us, aging leaves its subtle marks—dimming our eyes, shutting the doors of our hearing, causing our lips to tremble, turning our spirit of adventure into one of fear (see Eccles. 12:1–7). But when we are raised, we will be imperishable (1 Cor. 15:42b). Our vibrant colors will never again be muted with the brush of old age.

2. **Dishonorable versus glorious.** Our present bodies are not only perishable, they're dishonorable; our future bodies, not only imperishable but glorious. Although sown in the soil of sin, bearing the thorns of lustful drives and fleshly impulses, they will be raised in innocent glory (v. 43a).

3. **Weak versus powerful.** William Barclay captures Paul's thought behind this contrast (v. 43b).

> It is nowadays fashionable to talk of man's power, but the really remarkable thing is his weakness. A draught of air or a drop of water can kill him. We are limited in this life so often simply because of the necessary limitations of the body. Time

and time again our physical constitution says to
our visions and our plans, "Thus far and no far-
ther." We are so often frustrated because we are
what we are. But in the life to come the limitations will be gone. Here we are compassed about
with weakness; there we will be clad with power.
"All we have hoped or willed or dreamed
    of good shall exist;
The high that proved too high, the
    heroic for earth too hard."[2]
4. **Natural versus spiritual.** Paul makes a final contrast in
verse 44a.

It is sown a natural body, it is raised a spiritual
body.

In our natural bodies, we're dominated by the desires of our
natural man, desires we must constantly squelch (Rom.
7:14–25). But in our future, spiritual bodies, we will be dominated by the power of the Holy Spirit and therefore live as
Christ lives—in complete holiness and submission to the
Father. In fact, we will be like Christ physically (1 John 3:2)—
able to do everything He did in His resurrected body (see
John 20:19–29, Luke 24:33–43)—and completely free from
sickness, sadness, and death (Rev. 21:4).

C. **Adam and Christ.** Paul wraps up his reply to the Corinthians
with a quick comparison/contrast of Adam and Christ.

If there is a natural body, there is also a spiritual body.
So also it is written, "The first man, Adam, became a
living soul." The last Adam became a life-giving spirit.
However, the spiritual is not first, but the natural;
then the spiritual. The first man is from the earth,
earthy; the second man is from heaven. As is the
earthy, so also are those who are earthy; and as is the
heavenly, so also are those who are heavenly. And just
as we have borne the image of the earthy, we shall
also bear the image of the heavenly. (1 Cor. 15:44b–49)

Adam and Christ have at least two things in common: their
beginnings were both unique and sinless. But what they accomplished was altogether different. Formed from the dust of the
ground, Adam gave *natural* life to the entire human race. But,
conceived by the Spirit, Jesus is able to give *spiritual* life to all
who believe (1 John 4:9, 5:11; Rom. 8:2, 10).[3]

2. William Barclay, *The Letters to the Corinthians,* rev. ed., The Daily Study Bible Series (Philadelphia, Pa.: Westminster Press, 1975), p. 158.

3. For a more thorough explanation of Adam as a type of Christ, see Romans 5:12–21.

> ### Changing Your Image
> Bearing Adam's image, we're all destined to die (see Rom. 5:12). But if we also bear the image of Christ, we will live forever (v. 17).
>
> Have you changed your image from the natural to the spiritual? Does your life reflect Adam's image or Christ's? Does it mirror glory instead of guilt?

III. Our Present Bodies

Hopefully, Paul's discussion has addressed some of your questions about our resurrection bodies. But before we're through, let's consider the value of our present bodies—something we all need to be reminded of.

A. God designed your body for *you*, so accept it as it is. In accepting the body God has given you, you embrace His sovereignty and grace in your life. You say yes to part of His plan for you, and you begin to value what He values (see Matt. 6:25–32, Ps. 139:13–15, Luke 12:6–7). If He gives each tiny seed a body suited especially for it (1 Cor. 15:38), think about how much more skill He uses in creating our bodies.

B. God planned the distinctions between you and others, so don't compare yourself to someone else. Playing the comparison game—with occupations, grades, looks, gifts— is a no-win situation. Remember, "all flesh is not the same flesh" (v. 39a). You're unique! So relax. Be content with how He's made you—enjoy yourself exactly as you are.

C. God predicted that your body would have certain limitations, so stop condemning yourself. Since we all bear an earthly image, it's unrealistic to expect perfection. If you're condemning yourself because of a nagging sin, confess it and move on (1 John 1:9). Often, the last step in experiencing forgiveness from God is having the grace to forgive yourself.

Living Insights

Our future bodies—a subject that should capture everyone's interest. Paul has had much to say about this, much that's worth remembering and applying.

- One of the best ways to take the Scriptures to heart is to put them in your own words. This is called paraphrasing. Take this time to write anew Paul's words from 1 Corinthians 15:35–49. As you do, be free in expanding the passage's meanings, and pay attention to the deep feelings you may be discovering in the text . . . and in yourself.

1 Corinthians 15:35–49

_____

_____

_____

_____

_____

_____

_____

_____

_____

_____

_____

_____

_____

_____

_____

_____

_____

Continued on next page

_____

_____

_____

_____

_____

_____

_____

 Living Insights

Study Two ▬▬▬▬▬▬▬▬▬▬▬▬▬▬▬▬▬▬▬▬▬▬▬

Discontentment, comparison, and condemnation are all contrary to God's plan and design for you. Yet these are areas of constant struggle for many Christians. Bring together a group of friends or family and discuss these issues. Use the following questions as a springboard, and encourage everyone to participate... accept everybody's comments.

- Why do you think people are unwilling to accept the bodies God gave them?
- Do you think our society encourages comparison? Why or why not?
- Comparison can be a sign of insecurity. Do you agree or disagree? Why?
- In general, do you feel that people are too hard on themselves or too easy?
- How can God's grace impact these areas?

The Greatest Mystery Ever Told

1 Corinthians 15:50–58

One of the benefits of belonging to any family, group, or club is being able to be in on the secrets.

Only family members know exactly which spices Mom uses in her home-made spaghetti sauce. Only those who have credit with a major department store receive fliers in the mail announcing the upcoming, one-day-only, blowout sale. And only those who've been initiated into a particular sorority know the meaning of the club's Greek motto.

It's the same way with those of us who belong to God. Because we've been born into His spiritual clan, we have the benefit of being in on some of the family secrets.

In 1 Corinthians 15:50–58, Paul cups his hands to his mouth and, into the ears of the believers at Corinth, reveals a mystery,[1] a family secret—whispered to him by the very mouth of God.[2]

I. The Question behind the Mystery

Before revealing the mystery, Paul answers an underlying question. He has already explained that the dead in Christ will be raised and described the nature of their resurrection bodies (1 Cor. 15:35–49). But what about those who are still alive on that resurrection day? Will they remain in their earthly bodies? This must have nagged at the Corinthians' minds. So Paul supplies the answer, beginning in verse 50.

> Now I say this, brethren, that flesh and blood cannot inherit the kingdom of God; nor does the perishable inherit the imperishable.

Like caterpillars who can't fly until they've been transformed, so we will never see heaven unless our bodies are changed.

II. The Mystery Revealed

On the heels of this thought, Paul begins to tell the secret—the event of the Rapture.

---

1. Here *mystery* doesn't convey the idea of something that's confusing or hard to understand, but of something not known by the uninitiated, something that cannot be known without assistance—a secret.

2. In his commentary on 1 Corinthians, David Prior explains that Paul "suggests strongly that what he is saying has been unveiled to him by special revelation." See *The Message of 1 Corinthians: Life in the Local Church* (Downers Grove, Ill.: InterVarsity Press, 1985), p. 275.

In the event of Christ's return this driver will disappear. and the car will self destruct. ~secret

1st floor.
ch 4.

Behold, I tell you a mystery; we shall not all sleep,[3] but
we shall all be changed. (v. 51) ~mystery mystery

Here Paul says that what happened to the dead in Christ will happen
to the living. Transformation . . . change. Commentator Frederic Godet
clarifies this point.

disease
deform

> It is so impossible that the present body should partici-
> pate in the life of heaven, that, whether dissolved by
> death or not, it must be transformed.[4]

In verses 52–57, Paul details this transformation.

Check out line
Drivers license

A. **The Rapture's suddenness.** It will occur "in a moment, in
the twinkling of an eye" (v. 52a). Derived from the Greek word
atomos, the word *moment* conveys the idea of something that
cannot be divided, separated, or added on to. The other example
he gives—the flutter of an eyelid or a flash of light reflected in
someone's eye—also expresses the extreme suddenness of the
Rapture. *Moon - 2 sec   1st Star - 4 yrs.*

B. **The Rapture's order.** Also, the Rapture will occur
> at the last trumpet; for the trumpet will sound,[5] and
> the dead will be raised imperishable, and we shall
> be changed. (v. 52b)   *living*

Heralded by the resonant sound of the last trumpet, dead believers will be raised first, and then the living, changed. But
whether living or dead, we who believe will "meet the Lord in the
air, and thus *we shall always be with the Lord*" (1 Thess. 4:17b,
emphasis added; see also vv. 15–18).

C. **The Rapture's necessities.** Paul now gives us two events
that must happen before we can enjoy the presence of the Lord.
> For this perishable must put on the imperishable, and
> this mortal must put on immortality. (1 Cor. 15:53)

Like trying to mix oil with water, combining heaven with death
and decay just won't work. Not only *will* we all be changed
(v. 51b)—we *must.*

D. **The Rapture's victory.** Paul goes on to explain what will
happen after the transformation.
> But when this perishable will have put on the imper-
> ishable, and this mortal will have put on immortality,

3. The Lord never uses the words *sleep* or *asleep* to refer to the death of the unsaved—but
instead uses words such as *perished, lost, without hope, condemned,* and *under wrath.* Only
the person who knows Christ and has died is described as "asleep."

4. Frederic Louis Godet, *Commentary on First Corinthians* (1889; reprint, Grand Rapids, Mich.:
Kregel Publications, 1977), p. 862.

5. In Bible times, trumpets were used to assemble people, signal God's presence, or declare
that the end is near (Exod. 19:16–19, Isa. 27:13, Joel 2:1, Matt. 24:29–31). Each of these purposes
is in view in this passage.

Last trumpet— Egypt to palestine Journey. lots of people
canaan.   2 x 10⁶.
Communication lines drawn — Cloud + fire moved.
Trumpets were used for commun.   7th trumpet moved out!!
Last trumpet

Greek word — something not known by ministry uninitiated, secret fraternity
Jesus has a fraternity

then will come about the saying that is written, "Death *theology* is swallowed up in victory. O death, where is your *Isaiah* victory? O death, where is your sting?" (vv. 54–55)
Ever since the days of Adam and Eve, death has strutted around, the proud victor. It has played no favorites. Given no warning. Known no season of the year. But after the Rapture, never again will anyone grieve the loss of a loved one. Never again. For death's sting will be permanently gone. Paul begins to explain why in verse 56.

The sting of death is sin, and the power of sin is the law.

Through sin, death gains its authority over man. And by the Law, sin is strengthened. God's Law—the prohibitions, the thou-shalt-nots—actually gives sin power. This doesn't mean that the Law is sinful, as Paul clarifies in Romans 7:7.

What shall we say then? Is the Law sin? May it never be! On the contrary, I would not have come to know sin except through the Law; for I would not have known about coveting if the Law had not said, "You shall not covet."

Paul's point is that a warning often prompts a wrong. You've experienced it. You read the sign next to a pond that says, Positively No Fishing. And what do you get a sudden hankering to do? Fish in the pond! But sin and death won't always have their luring way with us. As Paul writes:

But thanks be to God, who gives us the victory through our Lord Jesus Christ. (1 Cor. 15:57)

It is at the Rapture that our victory over sin and death will become more than a taste. It will be completely ours!

III. Our Response to the Mystery

Now that we've heard the secret Paul whispered to the Corinthians centuries ago, what are we to do? Set dates for the Rapture? Quit our jobs, sell our possessions, sit on a hilltop and wait? No, Jesus told us that no one except the Father knows the season, day, or hour of His return (Matt. 24:36, 42; Acts 1:6–7). The answer is given in Paul's final thoughts, thoughts that are meant to encourage and edify us.

Therefore, my beloved brethren, be steadfast, immovable, always abounding in the work of the Lord, knowing that your toil is not in vain in the Lord. (1 Cor. 15:58)

What is the "work of the Lord"? It's the fulfillment of God's will for your life. But God's will is seldom cut-and-dried—it does not necessarily mean being a missionary, pastor, or Christian schoolteacher. It is something designed to fit your own unique abilities and gifts.

But whatever it is, He wants you to be committed—rocklike—to that will. In a nutshell, Paul is saying, "Live each day as if it were your last."

The Last Days

Do you live as if today were the last chance you had to invest time in life's most significant things? Would you spend your time as you do now if you knew that tomorrow you'd hear that last trumpet sound?

The secret's out. He *is* coming back; we will all be raised completely sinless to spend eternity with Him. When He does come, will He find you abounding in His work? Or will it look as though you've forgotten to prepare for the Rapture, the greatest mystery ever told?

 ## Living Insights

Study One ━━━━━━━━━━━━━━━━━━━━━━━━━━━━━━━━━━━━

This chapter closes with a passage that's vital to understanding future events. With the assistance of cross-references, let's put together a well-defined look at the greatest mystery ever told.

- Listed below are some key texts for understanding what is ahead in God's timetable. Carefully read each passage; then record your observations. When you've finished with this, try writing a summary paragraph that pulls all the information together.

The Greatest Mystery Ever Told

1 Corinthians 15:51–57 _____

_____

_____

1 Thessalonians 4:13–18 _____

_____

_____

John 14:1–3 _____

_____

_____

Summary

_____

_____

_____

_____

_____

_____

_____

_____

_____

_____

 Living Insights

Study Two

So much in this chapter gives us great cause for rejoicing! The child of God is rich indeed. And the greatest treasure of all is a copy of God's own Word—the Bible.

- Select a verse or a passage from 1 Corinthians 15 and memorize it. Perhaps you'll choose verse 58 for its encouragement. Or maybe verses 1–4 for their wonderful summary of the gospel. Or verses 13–14 for the supreme importance of the Resurrection. Memorizing is an excellent way to take the riches of God with you wherever you go. What a super way to apply the truths of Scripture!

"Now Concerning the Collection"
1 Corinthians 16:1-4

Money has been called the substance that can buy us everything but happiness and take us everywhere but heaven.

In fact, money can't buy you a lot of things. It may buy you a stack of books and pay your tuition to the finest university, but it cannot buy you the intellect with which to learn. Money may buy you all sorts of medicines and doctors, but it cannot buy you health. It may buy you a million-dollar house with an ocean view, but it can't even come close to buying you a home. It may buy you companionship, associates with big names and important titles, but not the love of a friend. Money can get you a solid-gold crucifix, but it cannot get you a Savior. The really important things in life simply aren't for sale.

This isn't to say that money is not important, even vital—especially to the Lord's work. If believers stopped giving, Christian organizations would fold. Mission fields would be vacant. Books would no longer be published. Churches would shut their doors. And believers themselves would miss out on one of the greatest blessings in life.

I. The Subject

In 1 Corinthians 16:1–4, Paul puts his finger on the importance of financial giving—a topic that in some churches is overkilled, and in others, ignored.

A. The matter in question. You can almost see the grimaces on the Corinthians' faces as they reach this part of Paul's letter.

Now concerning the collection for the saints. (v. 1a)

Notice the article *the* before the words *collection* and *saints.* From his choice of words, we understand that Paul had a *particular* collection in mind. He's not talking about regular giving, but giving to a specific project over and above their usual gifts. This would not go into the general fund, but to a special group of saints in Jerusalem (v. 3).[1]

B. The need for the collection. The early Church was conceived in the outpouring of the Holy Spirit on the day of Pentecost (Acts 2), and the local churches that sprung from her members were the fruit of her womb. But the church in Jerusalem, though the firstborn, suffered from some postnatal problems that threatened its life. Soon after birth a severe famine struck,

---

1. Also, the word Paul uses for *collection* is *logeia,* meaning "*an extra collection* . . . something which was the opposite of a tax which a man had to pay; it was an extra piece of giving." From *The Letters to the Corinthians,* rev. ed., The Daily Study Bible Series, by William Barclay (Philadelphia, Pa.: Westminster Press, 1975), p. 163.

hitting the church in Jerusalem especially hard (Acts 11:27–30) and leaving many of its members starving. Paul's heart bled for these people, so he organized a relief effort, calling upon the church at Corinth to help meet the needs of her mother church.

Expressing and Meeting Financial Needs

Paul's openness about the collection brings up two points we can all apply.

First, it's not wrong to let your financial needs be known. Many have a strong conviction against making monetary matters public; others just feel deeply uncomfortable. But as we see in this passage, Paul quite candidly carried the news of Jerusalem's situation to the congregations at Corinth and Galatia (1 Cor. 16:1). We, too, should feel free to express our financial needs, giving God the opportunity to lighten our load through the generosity of others. Also, like Paul, we should be sensitive to others' needs and offer an outstretched hand when we are able.

Paul makes another important point. Our giving should not be limited to our own local church. Our primary place of blessing should be our main place of giving—but not the *only* place. Ministries that regularly feed our souls or touch our hearts should also benefit from our financial gifts.

II. The Principles

After making his plea for the church at Jerusalem, Paul lays down several principles in verse 2 that apply to our special offerings as well as our regular giving.

A. Giving should be systematic. Paul urges the Corinthians to set aside money for their offerings "on the first day of every week." Giving shouldn't be done haphazardly. It should be done with thoughtful, regular planning. How careful are you about planning? Do you communicate this discipline to your family?

B. Giving should be an individual matter. Paul also says, "Let *each* one of you" support the Church financially, not just the wealthy . . . the long-standing members . . . the teachers . . . the adults. *Everybody* is to be involved in giving. Are you contributing to the financial health of the Body of Christ—including your own local church? Do you see that your individual gift is significant to the whole Body?

C. Giving is to be consistent. Paul tells the Corinthians to "put aside and save"—literally, "*keep* putting aside and saving."

Their giving was to be a consistent, regular part of their service and worship. Do you support your church regularly, consistently enjoying the benefits and delights of giving?

D. Giving is to be proportionate to what we receive. Paul now states one of the most important principles of giving:

Let each one of you put aside and save, *as he may prosper.* (emphasis added)

Each week we are to see how much we have received and use that as a basis for determining how much we should give. The amount of our paychecks may differ, but we should all have the same attitude toward giving.

Let each one do just as he has purposed in his heart; not grudgingly or under compulsion; for *God loves a cheerful giver.* (2 Cor. 9:7, emphasis added)[2]

Do you give cheerfully? Or, when the offering plate is passed, do you have to forcibly remove your whitened knuckles from around your check?

Grace and Tithing

Curiously, Paul, the New Testament writer who spoke most frequently on the topic of giving, never mentioned tithing. He had plenty of opportunities to explain this custom, because many of his readers were Gentiles who were unfamiliar with Jewish traditions. But since neither he nor any other New Testament writer commanded believers to give 10 percent of their earnings, we can conclude that we aren't obligated to tithe. Instead, we have the opportunity to give as the Lord lays it on our hearts. Grace-giving, not tithing, is the task God has given us.[3]

This isn't to say that tithing is outdated. It just means tithing should be motivated by grace, not law. Giving should be something between you and God—and something always done joyfully!

E. Giving should be a private matter. Paul didn't want his presence to pressure the Corinthians into giving, so he asked "that no collections be made when I come" (1 Cor. 16:2c)—that the knot on the offering bag be tied by the time he came to

---

2. The Greek word for *cheerful* means "hilarious." God loves a giver who finds joy in supporting His work.

3. For more information on grace-giving versus tithing, see Lawrence O. Richards's book *Expository Dictionary of Bible Words* (Grand Rapids, Mich.: Zondervan Publishing House, 1985), pp. 307–10.

receive it. When you put your gift in the plate, it doesn't matter whether others hear the rustle of a few large bills or the clink of loose change. Your giving is a private matter between you and God (Matt. 6:1–4). No reason to feel proud, no reason to feel ashamed. It's just you privately giving back to God a portion of His blessing to you.

III. The Arrangements

Paul's closing comments on the collection concern the transport of the Corinthians' gift to the church in Jerusalem.

> And when I arrive, whomever you may approve, I shall send them with letters to carry your gift to Jerusalem; and if it is fitting for me to go also, they will go with me.
> (1 Cor. 16:3–4)

Paul was particularly discreet when it came to handling the Corinthian church's money. He wanted no part in collecting it, counting it, or delivering it. He would, however, put his seal of approval on whomever they chose to deliver it, accompanying them himself if the gift was large enough. Other than encouraging them to give, he kept his hands out of their money matters. Unfortunately, Paul's plea went unheeded. The affluent Corinthians clutched their wallets tightly, while the poorer congregation of Macedonia dug deep into their pockets and gave . . . and gave . . . and gave (2 Cor. 8:1–4). What made the difference? Unlike the self-centered Corinthians, the generous Macedonians "first gave themselves to the Lord" (v. 5). God's goals were their primary concern, so they found it easy to give exuberantly. What kind of giver are you?

IV. Some Concluding Thoughts

Here are a few tips to help us balance our spiritual checkbooks.

A. **Giving is not dependent on the size of your church, but on the conviction of your heart.** The amount you give ought to be determined by you and the Lord, not by how big your congregation is. Surprisingly, large and wealthy congregations are often out-given by smaller ones. So we shouldn't allow a church's size to dictate how much we contribute to its ministry. Giving is not a matter of numbers—it's a matter of the heart.

B. **Giving must be prompted from within, not pressured from without.** We shouldn't wait for slick gimmicks, contests, or emotional sales pitches to motivate our giving. We should realize that ministries have ongoing expenses and establish a habit of giving. And, like the Macedonian church, we should be ready to meet special needs—even if it means giving sacrificially.

C. Giving is an important way to gauge your gratitude.
Warren Wiersbe says it well:

> Christian giving is a *grace,* the outflow of the grace
> of God in our lives and not the result of promotion
> or pressure. An open heart cannot maintain a closed
> hand. If we appreciate the grace of God extended to
> us, we will want to express that grace by sharing with
> others.[4]

As James tells us, "Every good thing bestowed and every perfect
gift is from above, coming down from the Father of lights, with
whom there is no variation, or shifting shadow" (1:17). If you're
thankful for the many gifts with which God's blessed you, show
Him your gratitude by sharing your blessings with others. Live
your life by Jesus' command (Matt. 10:8b): " 'Give as freely as
you have received!' "[5]

 Living Insights

Study One ▬▬▬▬▬▬▬▬▬▬▬▬▬▬▬▬▬▬▬▬▬▬▬▬▬▬▬▬

Mention money and suddenly you have everybody's attention. It's
one of those subjects that generates interest without even trying. Do
you know what Scripture says about money . . . giving . . . the collection?
Let's take a few minutes to examine these important issues.

- With the help of a concordance, locate key biblical passages refer-
  ring to giving, tithing, the collection, and money. Use the chart that
  follows to record your findings. What do these verses tell you? Is giving different in the New Testament than in the Old? What is required
  of us today?

"Now Concerning the Collection"	
Passages	Observations

---

4. Warren W. Wiersbe, *Be Wise* (Wheaton, Ill.: Victor Books, 1983), p. 163.

5. The Living Bible (Wheaton, Ill.: Tyndale House Publishers, 1971).

Passages	Observations

 Living Insights

Study Two ▬▬▬▬▬▬▬▬▬▬▬▬▬▬▬▬▬

One of the best ways to chart your spiritual growth is to go back and examine your checkbook. You may not have thought of it this way, but your checkbook is actually a spiritual journal that demonstrates your priorities in no uncertain terms. After all, as Jesus said in Matthew 6:21, "Where your treasure is, there will your heart be also."

- Use this time to analyze your financial practices. Do your money matters glorify God? Do you design your budget with the awareness that it all belongs to Him? How does that fact demonstrate itself in your everyday financial affairs? Are you actively involved in giving to God-honoring ministries, with your local church as your highest priority? Carefully think through issues like these and, if they apply, make some changes in the way you handle your money—starting today.

ABCs of One-on-One

You remember them. Those sweltering school-day afternoons when the steady hum of the old metal fan almost lulled you to sleep.

Slouched in your seat, you tried to listen to the teacher explain long division; but despite all your earnest efforts, it didn't quite sink in. A sparrow hopping from branch to branch on the maple tree outside the window kept catching your eye, the boy in front of you kept clicking his pen on the desk top, and the teacher's perplexing lecture sounded like fingernails scratching across the blackboard of your mind.

After the final bell had rung and all the other kids had gone home, you asked your teacher to explain the material again. The teacher pulled a chair up to your desk, picked up your pencil, and showed you, step-by-step, how to work the problems—until you were able to work each one on your own.

As in the classroom, so in our Christian walk we learn best when we're not only told, but shown—when somebody pulls us from the church pews, seminar halls, and bookstores and disciples us one-on-one through the everyday disciplines of the Christian life.

That's how we become best equipped with the skills to live the good news of Jesus victoriously. And, consequently, how we are best able to spread the good news so that others will decide to follow Him too.

I. Jesus: The Master Discipler

Look at Jesus. He could've peppered the hills of Jerusalem with fliers telling who He was or held tent meetings every night of His three-year ministry. But He virtually ignored the idea of classrooming the masses. Instead, He pulled up a chair next to twelve men—hand-picked one by one—to pour Himself into them so that they might spread His truth to others, and those to still others . . . until it had snowballed and the whole world had heard the good news.

> And He went up to the mountain and summoned those whom He Himself wanted, and they came to Him. And He appointed twelve, that they might be with Him, and that He might send them out to preach. (Mark 3:13–14)

Jesus spent time with His disciples, teaching them to live the Christian life. And in His last words to them, He gave a command that would echo in their hearts long after their last glimpse of His face had faded.

> "Go therefore and make disciples of all the nations, baptizing them in the name of the Father and the Son and the

80

Holy Spirit, teaching them to observe all that I commanded
you; and lo, I am with you always, even to the end of the
age." (Matt. 28:19–20)
And after He left, they picked up the torch and set the world on fire
with His message.

II. Paul: One of the Master's Best Students

Paul, like Christ, was a teacher diligently committed to his students.
The classroom at Corinth was struggling; they needed someone to
show them firsthand how to follow God. In 1 Corinthians 16:5–12,
we see Paul volunteering to tutor them, with Timothy's help. In this
passage Paul chalks out six principles of discipleship for believers
everywhere to follow.

**A. Discipleship starts with those who know where they're
going.** Paul laid out an itinerary for himself. He had planned
to visit Macedonia (v. 5), then travel on to Corinth. And even
though some of the Corinthians were critical, saying he would
never make it to Corinth (4:18), he stuck to his plan of action.
Like the children of Israel, led by the cloud and the pillar of fire,
Paul had a strong sense of purpose and direction in his life.

> **Knowing and Showing the Way**
>
> The Lord Jesus—the quintessential teacher—knew exactly where He was going. His confidence attracted a group
> of hardened fishermen, ill-trained for His kind of work, to
> put down their nets and follow Him. He was even able to
> pluck Matthew from the ranks of the hated tax gatherers
> and turn his life around, pointing him with a spiritual compass in the right direction. Jesus knew where He was going.
> And, magnetically, drew others to follow Him.
>
> What about you? Is your life guided by the Holy Spirit's
> itinerary? Do you know the way well enough to be followed?

**B. Discipleship means getting personally involved for
an extended period of time.** Like a tutor who commits to
helping a student throughout the whole semester, Paul was ready
to commit himself to the Corinthians for an entire season. He
tells them:

> And perhaps I shall stay with you, or even spend the
> winter, that you may send me on my way wherever
> I may go. For I do not wish to see you now just in
> passing; for I hope to remain with you for some time,
> if the Lord permits. (vv. 6–7)

The word for *with* in these verses carries the idea of intimate involvement, face-to-face contact and dialogue.[1] Paul's visit to Corinth wasn't prompted by a desire to take a quick tour of the city's sights; he wanted to stay *with them* and, for a substantial period of time, be an intimate part of their lives.

> ## Face-to-Face
> After Jesus called His disciples, one of the first things He did was take some of them home with Him (John 1:38–39), letting them past the porch of His life. He knew that disciples aren't developed by proxy, that it takes a long-term, intimate relationship . . . eyeball-to-eyeball, face-to-face.
>
> Are you willing to spend the time necessary to help build the spiritual foundations of others? Willing to become part of the brick and mortar of their lives?

C. **Discipleship is sustained by the Lord's permission.** Notice how Paul hinges his visit on one condition: "If the Lord permits" (v. 7b).[2] If God doesn't give him the go-ahead, Paul will change his plans. He is determined not to force the situation, but to rely on God's timing. For Paul, discipleship was a way of life. From his example we see that it isn't learned in the classroom, there are no mechanical formulas to follow, and it isn't even in our hands to choose when or whom we will disciple. God is the one who links lives in the bond of discipleship—both permitting it and keeping it alive.

D. **Discipleship flourishes in the context of unguarded honesty.** In verses 8–9, Paul bares his heart to the believers at Corinth.

> But I shall remain in Ephesus until Pentecost; for a wide door for effective service has opened to me, and there are many adversaries.

Paul wasn't embarrassed to share about God's blessings or his own struggles. Without a trace of pride, he told them that great things were happening in Ephesus. And, without a trace of shame, that he was struggling (see also 2 Cor. 1:8–10). Transparent, he wanted them to know his heart.

---

1. John used this term in John 1:1 when he referred to Jesus—the Word—as *with* God.

2. The Greek word for *permits, epitrepō,* conveys the idea of a person's wanting something badly, even longing for it, but waiting for the Lord to make it possible.

E. Discipleship is strengthened through mutual support and equal respect. To Paul, there was no such thing as a spiritual giant. He reminded the Corinthians that all God's spokesmen are to be respected equally.

> Now if Timothy comes, see that he is with you without cause to be afraid; for he is doing the Lord's work, as I also am. Let no one therefore despise him. But send him on his way in peace, so that he may come to me; for I expect him with the brethren. (1 Cor. 16:10–11)

Here Paul warns them not to reject Timothy because of his youth and inexperience (see also 1 Tim. 4:12), not to feel that Timothy was second-best. Because Paul and Timothy were both doing the Lord's work, they both deserved equal support and respect. In the same way, the relationship between the discipler and the person being discipled is to be marked by reciprocal encouragement and esteem.

F. Discipleship must allow room for disagreement and individualism. In 1 Corinthians 16:12, Paul closes his series of principles.

> But concerning Apollos our brother, I encouraged him greatly to come to you with the brethren; and it was not at all his desire to come now, but he will come when he has opportunity.

Paul's associate, Apollos, declined to visit Corinth despite Paul's urging. But notice that Paul didn't get angry. Honoring Apollos's individuality, Paul gave him room to make his own decisions. We ought to be doing this in all aspects of our Christian walk, but especially in the realm of discipleship. New believers can grow up in Christ only as they are allowed the freedom to think for themselves.

    The goal of the discipleship curriculum isn't to make clones out of the classroomed masses, but to nurture individuals.
    And you can do this most effectively when you invest your time in showing others, up close, the Jesus in your life.

Living Insights

Study One ■■■■■■■■■■■■■■■■■■■■■■■■■■■■■■■■■■■■

    Our lesson showed six principles of discipleship. If you've been discipled, in what ways were these six principles lived out and how were you affected? If you've been thinking about discipling someone, how would you put each of these principles to work?

- Listed below are the six principles from our lesson. Use the space provided to crystallize your thoughts on these statements. If discipleship has never been a part of your life, that's OK. Why don't you take time now to pray about this and ask God to show you how discipleship could be brought into your life.

1. Discipleship starts with those who know where they're going.

_____

_____

_____

2. Discipleship means getting personally involved for an extended period of time.

_____

_____

_____

3. Discipleship is sustained by the Lord's permission.

_____

_____

_____

4. Discipleship flourishes in the context of unguarded honesty.

_____

_____

_____

5. Discipleship is strengthened through mutual support and equal respect.

_____

_____

_____

6. Discipleship must allow room for disagreement and individualism.

_____

_____

_____

 Living Insights

If you have been discipled and were able to see those principles personified in the ones who discipled you, you are a very fortunate person indeed. In a day when so many new Christians are abandoned on the doorstep, nurturing disciplers are a vanishing breed.

- Write some letters of thanks to those who discipled you. Share your gratitude for their manifesting the character traits described in this lesson, and let them know that the time spent was not in vain. Bring them up to date on your walk with the Lord. And if you haven't been discipled and would like to be, take this time to contact a leader at your church who could help you find a discipler.

With All My Love . . . Paul

1 Corinthians 16:13–20

In every class of forty or so literature students, even the best teachers will kindle a flame of enthusiasm in only two or three. Many may feel a spark of casual interest, but only a few will be ignited.

But what joy the instructor feels when those few students take Dante, Shakespeare, or James Joyce out of the dim classroom and into the light of life—when they choose literature as their own field. Because these students and their teacher share a passion for understanding the ideas and ideals of mankind, they are soldered in an unbreakable bond.

In the same way, those few who have heard the good news of Jesus and who choose to follow Him passionately are welded to Him. They are interested in more than just acquiring the facts about Him; they have become one in purpose with Him, devoutly following in His footsteps.

Such students of Jesus are known as disciples. And that's what each of us has been called to be.

I. The Disciple's Reactions to Those outside Christ

In 1 Corinthians 16:13–14, Paul gives those who've chosen Jesus as their life's study a list of commands for responding to unbelievers. Not merely to be practiced in the classroom, these commands are to be lived out continually.

A. "Be on the alert" (v. 13a). With this phrase, Paul commands us to keep staying awake, keep watching, keep discerning. Jesus also used this phrase often; in fact, our Lord was consistently urging His disciples to stay awake, to listen up. You've probably heard it said that the world can be divided into three categories: the few who make things happen, the many who watch things happen, and the vast majority who have no idea what in the world is happening. Paul warns us not to be characterized by the ignorance of the masses, but to always *be aware.*

Awareness Check

How alert are you to the needs around you?

Are you aware of the pressures, fears, and victories of those you brush lives with? Do you hear more than what is said . . . do you see more than what is obvious? Or, like a lethargic student, do you tend to fall asleep at your desk?

B. "Stand firm in the faith" (v. 13b). As students of Jesus, it isn't always easy to take what we've learned and stand firm in it. Often, Satan waits for us by the lockers and tries to rip away what we've learned before we've had a chance to live in those lessons. We must counter Satan's great debates with our faith. Paul uses the imagery of a physical battle to help prepare us for our spiritual struggles:

> Put on the full armor of God, that you may be able to stand firm against the schemes of the devil. For our struggle is not against flesh and blood, but against the rulers, against the powers, against the world forces of this darkness, against the spiritual forces of wickedness in the heavenly places. Therefore, take up the full armor of God, that you may be able to resist in the evil day, and having done everything, to stand firm. Stand firm therefore, having girded your loins with truth, and having put on the breastplate of righteousness, and having shod your feet with the preparation of the gospel of peace; in addition to all, taking up the shield of faith with which you will be able to extinguish all the flaming missiles of the evil one. And take the helmet of salvation, and the sword of the Spirit, which is the word of God. (Eph. 6:11–17)

The attacks will come. Will you be able to rebut Satan's flaming, icy tongue with the truths you've learned and practiced, or will you forget God's protective principles as soon as the bell rings?

C. **"Act like men"** (1 Cor. 16:13c). Next, Paul commands us to "grow up!"[1] We've got to push toward spiritual maturity, setting aside our self-centered, kindergarten ways (see 3:1–3a, Heb. 5:11–6:1a).

Your Spiritual Growth Chart

Christians who are constantly fussing, demanding their own rights, complaining because they're not properly recognized or people don't greet them as they should or they don't get enough applause for what they do—believers like these are run by an immature spirit.

Spiritual maturity can be charted in believers by their level of indifference to praise and blame. In the hearts of those living to serve the *Lord,* what others think of *them* matters very little.

---

1. The original Greek term means "to conduct one's self in a manly or courageous way." Fritz Rienecker, *A Linguistic Key to the Greek New Testament,* ed. Cleon L. Rogers, Jr. (Grand Rapids, Mich.: Zondervan Publishing House, 1980), p. 448.

What about you? Are you easily slighted? Like a baby to a bottle, do you cling to your rights? If so, it's time to grow up—time to graduate into a school of higher spiritual learning.

D. **"Be strong"** (v. 13d). This command echoes Paul's prayer for the believers at Ephesus:

> For this reason, I bow my knees before the Father, from whom every family in heaven and on earth derives its name, that He would grant you, according to the riches of His glory, to be strengthened with power through His Spirit in the inner man. (Eph. 3:14–16)

The strength to follow the Lord obediently isn't created by a Charles Atlas physique. It comes from a tough *inner* man—one strong enough to handle criticism and temptation, sturdy enough to hold you up when the rug gets pulled out from under you or when you are forced to stand alone.

E. **"Let all that you do be done in love"** (1 Cor. 16:14). Paul's final command adds depth to all the others. Without love, you won't be alert and discerning, but narrow and suspicious. If you stand firm without love, you'll be an isolated fanatic, ugly in temperament and intolerant toward the lost. Without love to balance your maturity, you'll be critical and harsh. And if you're strong yet have no love, you'll lack the tenderness that will cause others to be attracted to your strength. Notice the one characteristic Jesus said would identify His disciples. It wasn't discernment or a firm stand or maturity or strength—it was *love.*

> "By this all men will know that you are My disciples, if you have love for one another." (John 13:35)

The Meaning of Love

What does it mean to be really loved by somebody? It means being accepted.

Acceptance means being valued just as you are. It allows you to be yourself instead of forcing you into someone else's mold. It takes your thoughts seriously. It lets you express your ideas, even heretical ones, without being shot down. It makes you feel free from judgment . . . it lets you feel safe.

We all long to experience this kind of acceptance, but do we give it to others? Do you let this kind of love permeate all your relationships?

II. The Disciple's Reactions toward Those in Christ

Beginning in verse 15, Paul changes his focus from our responses to non-Christians to our treatment of fellow believers. And he changes his tone as well—from one that commands to one that pleads.

A. "Acknowledge such men" (v. 18b). Paul makes his first plea in verses 15–18.

> Now I urge you, brethren (you know the household of Stephanas, that they were the first fruits of Achaia, and that they have devoted themselves for ministry to the saints), that you also be in subjection to such men and to everyone who helps in the work and labors. And I rejoice over the coming of Stephanas and Fortunatus and Achaicus; because they have supplied what was lacking on your part. For they have refreshed my spirit and yours. Therefore *acknowledge such men.* (emphasis added)

The Greek term for *acknowledge* means "respect"—the kind of respect that leads to subjection. Paul urges the Corinthians to submit to the leadership of Stephanas, Fortunatus, and Achaicus purely because of their service to the church. His words should cause us to reevaluate our approach to selecting church leaders.

> We tend to give leadership to those who have received one particular kind of education, who have a measure of articulacy and general ability to think and speak on their feet, who measure up to worldly criteria of leadership.... [But what Paul says] indicates that the authentic, solid leadership of a local church will come from people who give themselves to serving the saints. Such leadership does not depend on education, qualifications, degrees, or natural charisma. It comes from the grace of God equipping his people with gifts which enable them to be servants of others in the fellowship of believers.[2]

B. "Greet one another with a holy kiss" (v. 20b). Paul closes with a request that makes many of us squirm in our pews.

> All the brethren greet you. Greet one another with a holy kiss. (v. 20)

William Barclay explains this lost, first-century custom:

> The kiss of peace was a lovely custom of the early Church.... It was apparently given at the end of the prayers and just before the congregation partook of the sacrament. It was the sign and symbol that they

---

2. David Prior, *The Message of 1 Corinthians: Life in the Local Church* (Downers Grove, Ill.: InterVarsity Press, 1985), p. 283.

sat at the table of love joined together in perfect love. . . . It was not given promiscuously. Certainly in later times it was not given between men and women, but between man and man, and woman and woman. Sometimes it was given not on the lips but on the hand. It came to be called simply "The Peace." Surely never did a church need to be recalled to that lovely custom more than this Church at Corinth, so torn with strife and dissension.[3]

In our stiff, hands-off society, many of us are afraid to touch other believers. Yet, we need to give affection freely—the squeeze of a hand, a friendly hug, a pat on the back. One of the best ways to show others our love is through the acceptance we whisper in a warm touch.

Called to Be His Disciples

In a sense, we're all in a spiritual classroom, with the Lord as our teacher.

Some choose to sit in the back row and goof off. Distracted, they never pay attention to the truth of salvation.

Others listen attentively, taking careful notes; but they forget it all as soon as they've taken the test. To them, salvation answers the questions in their minds, not their hearts.

Then there are those who hang on the Teacher's every word, digesting His lessons, letting them change their lives.

What kind of student are you choosing to be? Is your primary passion to learn His ways and follow in His steps?

 Living Insights

Study One

Ever notice how easy it is to overlook the last chapter of an epistle? A few greetings to people with strange names or the words "holy kiss" seem to signal our brains to begin the skim. This is most unfortunate. Let's give the final chapter of 1 Corinthians the attention it rightly deserves.

• Reread the twenty-four verses of 1 Corinthians 16 in the Bible you use most often. Then find a different version and read this same

---

3. William Barclay, *The Letters to the Corinthians,* rev. ed., The Daily Study Bible Series (Philadelphia, Pa.: Westminster Press, 1975), p. 168.

section again. Does the different version bring some freshness into the way you see this passage? Are you able to sense additional meanings and feelings? Don't hurry. Give your thirsty soul the chance to drink deeply from God's Word.

 ## Living Insights

Study Two ━━━━━━━━━━━━━━━━━━━━━━━━━━━━━━━━━━━━━━━

"Behold, how they love one another!" an eyewitness once wrote of New Testament-era Christians. Can this be said of you? What would lead a person to make that sort of statement about you?

• The issue of love in your life is a matter worthy of prayer. Take the time you usually set aside for Living Insights and use it for a talk with God. Focus on love. Pray for a life that reflects Christ's love for you. Ask God to give you the ability to demonstrate your love in specific ways, and pray for wisdom to hurdle the barriers that keep you from a love-filled life.

Anathema! Maranatha! Amen!
1 Corinthians 16:21–24

Harry Ironside was one of the most distinguished voices of Christian fundamentalism. The first half of this century saw him rise in popularity as a Bible teacher, evangelist, pastor, and author. Up through his final days, he was in great demand across the United States and around the world.

Harry Ironside was also virtually blind. Cataracts had gradually stolen his sight, but they never seemed to slow him down. Personal aides stepped in to accomplish tasks he could no longer perform, particularly the writing of his correspondence. Reluctant to relinquish the touch of a personal letter, however, Ironside never let a piece of mail reach the post office without scrawling his signature and a brief, thoughtful note.

Ironside's postscripts lent warmth to his correspondence, but they also put a stamp of authenticity on the contents.

Another of our spiritual ancestors had a similar problem and employed a similar solution—Paul. Galatians 4:15 and 6:11 indicate that Paul's eyesight was failing, and we know that he typically used an aide, or amanuensis, to pen his correspondence. And, like Ironside, Paul never failed to add his handwritten PS to every letter, including his first letter to the Corinthians.

I. A Final Review

Let's take a few moments to review 1 Corinthians and reflect on where we've been. Following Paul's initial greeting and words of praise (1:1–9), the apostle gets down to the business at hand. He penetrates the Corinthians' veneer of spirituality by exhorting them to stop being so selfish and divisive (1:10–4:21). Then he addresses three areas of disorder—moral, legal, and carnal—each of which was destroying the inner life of the church as well as its witness to the world (5:1–6:20). Throughout much of the remainder of the letter, Paul answers the Corinthians' questions about marriage and divorce (7:1–40), liberty and license (8:1–11:1), women and worship (11:2–34), spiritual gifts and Body life (12:1–14:40), death and resurrection (15:1–58), and giving and receiving (16:1–4). Then, just before he scrawls his final words, he relates some crucial principles of discipleship (vv. 5–12) and some important commands for disciples to follow (vv. 13–20). From beginning to end, he reaches out to the Corinthians as spiritual kin, urging them to live up to their family name.

II. Paul's Last Words

Now Paul brings his letter to a close with words that first shine like the rays of the sun, then roar thunder, and finally refresh like soft, cool rain.

A. The greeting. The first words from Paul's own hand are of warm greetings (v. 21). The root term of *greeting* means "to welcome warmly, to receive with an embrace." It indicates a physical show of affection between friends (compare v. 20). Paul has written some stern words to the Corinthians; but now, squinting his eyes, he takes his pen in hand to reassure them that they are welcome in his life as his friends. He refuses to allow their disagreements to strain their Christ-given bond.

Love Conquers Conflict
It's hard for us to handle disagreements as skillfully as Paul did. Too often, our confrontations leave broken splinters of resentment festering under our skin until they poison our relationships.

Are you nursing a grudge against someone, subtly feeding it with secret scraps of disapproval? Love can conquer conflict. But you won't experience its power until you release your frustration to the God of love.

B. The curse. Paul slips in a last-minute admonition in verse 22.

If anyone does not love the Lord, let him be accursed.

When Paul refers to our love for Christ, he usually uses the word *agapē,* which indicates love in its strongest, purest form. Here, however, for the only time in his New Testament writings, he uses the word *phileō,* which suggests warm, friendly affection. The requirement of this verse is not great; all it demands is simple appreciation for the Lord Jesus. But for those whose hearts refuse—*anathema!* Small requirement, large penalty. This word means serious business. In essence, it's a curse. It means to set these people aside as objects of God's wrath. Paul is not alone in giving this advice. Jesus gave the same counsel to His disciples as He sent them out to preach the gospel and heal the sick in the surrounding countryside.

"And into whatever city or village you enter, inquire who is worthy in it; and abide there until you go away. And as you enter the house, give it your greeting. And if the house is worthy, let your greeting of peace come upon it; but if it is not worthy, let your greeting of peace return to you. And whoever does not receive you, nor heed your words, as you go out of that house or that city, shake off the dust of your feet. Truly I say to you, it will be more tolerable for the land of Sodom and Gomorrah in the day of judgment, than for that city." (Matt. 10:11–15)

C. The watchword. The curse is followed by an Aramaic word, *maranatha* (1 Cor. 16:22b), meaning "Our Lord, come!" Paul didn't have to translate—his Greek-speaking readers knew what it meant. It had become a watchword among Christians for Jesus' return. Paul follows the curse with this word of hope, communicating the idea that when Christ comes back, He'll set things right.

1. For more information on Christ's soon return, see Robert G. Gromacki's "The Imminent Return of Jesus Christ," in *Grace Journal* (Fall 1965), pp. 1–23; and John F. Walvoord's *The Rapture Question,* rev. ed. (Grand Rapids, Mich.: Zondervan Publishing House, 1979), chap. 6.

D. The farewell. Paul has exhorted, refuted, and rebuked the Corinthians through much of his letter. When he comes to his good-bye, though, he opens his arms to give these believers two gifts that will comfort and encourage them.

> The grace of the Lord Jesus be with you. My love be with you all in Christ Jesus. Amen. (1 Cor. 16:23–24)

Grace and love are the two ingredients the Corinthians needed most. Nothing less could heal their divisions, correct their disorders, and restore their witness. Paul holds out these gifts as if to say, "I've had strong words for you in this letter, but remember—the Lord is merciful and forgiving toward you, and I love you all deeply." How those words must have soothed sore consciences! They were accepted, faults and all, by their Savior and by their teacher.

Acceptance Guaranteed

It's easy to love people when we approve of them—when their beliefs, status, conduct, or bank accounts measure up to our standards. But as far as Paul is concerned, anyone who receives God's grace deserves our love. After all, where would any of us be apart from the Lord's boundless mercy? If God loves us just the way we are, then how can we set standards for others?

III. Some Timeless Application

We may have come to the end of Paul's letter to the Corinthians, but we haven't finished applying its truths. Before moving on to our last lesson in this study, let's consider four life principles implied in Paul's parting words.

A. Disagreement should never override courtesy. Don't allow differences or offenses to drive a wedge between you and other Christians. Remember, we ourselves are not without sin. And Jesus warned that if we refuse to forgive others, God will withhold His forgiveness from us (Matt. 18:21–35). So, like Paul, extend an accepting embrace instead of shooting an icy stare.

B. Everyone is not equally deserving of our time and effort. We should pour our lives into those who are genuinely responsive to the Lord and His work. But when we run across those whose hearts are cold, we should back away and let God deal with them.

C. When everything seems futile, remember the watchword: maranatha! On any day, at any hour, Jesus could return. And when He does, He'll begin to right every wrong, heal every wound, and wipe away every tear.

D. The greatest gifts we can give are God's grace and our love. God's grace is made real to others through the love we offer. But unless we ourselves receive His gift of grace through His Son, we'll never be able to love as we can and should. Do you know Jesus as your personal Savior? If not, won't you place your trust in Him today? If you're already a child of His, be a clear channel for His grace and love. Let them flow through your life like a sparkling mountain stream, bringing refreshment to everyone you meet.

Living Insights

Study One

As the last few verses bring this great epistle to a close, let's use these Living Insights as a chance to review what we've learned so far. Educators agree, much learning takes place in review—sometimes more learning than the first time around!

• Listed below are the first fifteen lessons from this study. Go back over your notes and find one truth from each lesson that seems to stand out above the others in your mind. Take your time, letting these truths sink in to become a part of you.

Calm Answers for a Confused Church

One Head, One Body, Many Functions _____

_____

_____

Analogies from Anatomy _____

_____

_____

Love: The Greatest of All _____

_____

_____

What about Tongues in the Church Today? _____

_____

_____

An Answer to Confusion about Tongues _____

_____

_____

Back from the Dead! _____

_____

_____

What If There Were No Resurrection? _____

_____

_____

Christ's Unfinished Work _____

_____

_____

Living for Tomorrow, Today _____

_____

_____

Our Future Bodies _____

_____

_____

The Greatest Mystery Ever Told _____

_____

_____

"Now Concerning the Collection" _____

_____

_____

ABCs of One-on-One _____

_____

_____

Continued on next page

With All My Love . . . Paul _____

_____

_____

Anathema! Maranatha! Amen! _____

_____

_____

Living Insights

Reviewing where we've been is a great journey, isn't it? Just as we saw many life-giving truths in this study, we've also seen some life-changing ways to apply these truths. Let's continue our review by highlighting these applications.

• As you look over the lessons we have studied together, choose one application from each that had a particular impact on your life. A lot has happened over the last few weeks, hasn't it?

Calm Answers for a Confused Church

One Head, One Body, Many Functions _____

_____

_____

Analogies from Anatomy _____

_____

_____

Love: The Greatest of All _____

_____

_____

What about Tongues in the Church Today? _____

_____

_____

Continued on next page

With All My Love . . . Paul _____

_____

_____

Anathema! Maranatha! Amen! _____

_____

_____

Standing Alone When Opposed
Joshua 24:13–15

When faced with an enemy one-on-one, it's fairly easy to keep our guard up—we're suspicious, ready to stick up for our morals, ready to stand alone. But often, rather than making a ruthless attack, our opposition appears to be more like a group of friends having a party. At these times it takes prodigious strength to resist the invitation to come on over and join them—and often, instead of standing alone, we end up sitting with our friendly foes in the world's plush seat of sin. Adding a new twist to an old fable, "Said the Spider to the Fly" illustrates this well.

> Once a spider built a beautiful web in an old house. He kept it clean and shiny so that flies would patronize it. The minute he got a "customer" he would clean up on him so the other flies would not get suspicious.
>
> Then one day this fairly intelligent fly came buzzing by the clean spiderweb. Old man spider called out, "Come in and sit." But the fairly intelligent fly said, "No sir. I don't see other flies in your house, and I am not going in alone!"
>
> But presently he saw on the floor below a large crowd of flies dancing around on a piece of brown paper. He was delighted! He was not afraid if *lots* of flies were doing it. So he came in for a landing.
>
> Just before he landed, a bee zoomed by, saying, "Don't land there, stupid! That's flypaper!" But the fairly intelligent fly shouted back, "Don't be silly. Those flies are dancing. There's a big crowd there. Everybody's doing it. That many flies can't be wrong!" Well, you know what happened. He died on the spot.
>
> Some of us want to be with the crowd so badly that we end up in a mess. What does it profit a fly (or a person) if he escapes the *web* only to end up in the *glue?*[1] (emphasis added)

The believers at Corinth had gotten stuck in the flypaper of the world's system. Dancing around on a surface sticky with immorality, selfishness, pleasure, pride, they flirted with the world's philosophies, inviting the kiss of death.

We, too, live in a society that beckons our allegiance. We must always be alert, for the world constantly lures us to come on over and join the

---

This message was not a part of the original series but is compatible with it.

1. "Said the Spider to the Fly," source unknown.

ranks. In this lesson we will discover how to stand alone when opposed by our society—how to beat the world's webby system and remain free.

I. Crucial Questions regarding the World's System

Before we can beat the system we must understand the stuff of its web—who has spun it, why it's been spun, and just how it can catch us.

A. Who is behind it? The eight-legged creature calling us to come sit in his web is none other than Satan.

We know that we are of God, and the whole world lies in the power of the evil one. (1 John 5:19)

What he offers as a winsome invitation to blissful rest is actually a proposal of death.

B. What are its objectives? The web of the world's system is spun with the thin, silken threads of fortune, fame, power, and pleasure. The world's ultimate goal is to get you to believe the lie that these will bring you security . . . and to leave you entangled in the web, limbs wriggling, caught.

1. **Fortune.** To build one's security on money is to live dangerously—the nice little nest egg you've been planning your future around just might break while it's still in the nest. Through the pen of the wise man Solomon, the Lord sketches the truth about money:

When you set your eyes on it, it is gone.
For wealth certainly makes itself wings,
Like an eagle that flies toward the heavens.
(Prov. 23:5; see also 11:28, 13:7)

2. **Fame.** Hollywood's glitzy glamour. Names marqueed in bold letters and bright lights. Being seen. Being known. These are the lures of the god of fame. But through the telescopic lens of reality we see that stars usually fall from their luminous heights of popularity, or they at least lose their shine. Diamonds may glisten on their fingers, but their eyes, the jewels of the soul, are lackluster and vacant.

Being Known

What greater joy than to be known by the One who has saved you!

Whether or not you ever see your name in print or your face on the screen, you're known. The Father has etched your name in His Book of Life and an imprint of your soul on His heart.

---

3. **Power.** In our dog-eat-dog world, society barks the orders "Take charge! Assert yourself! If you don't, you'll get walked

on. If you don't, you'll never get ahead. If you don't, . . ." But Jesus stands by and with tender authority says:
"Whoever exalts himself shall be humbled; and whoever humbles himself shall be exalted."
(Matt. 23:12)
Therefore, as James advises,
Humble yourselves in the presence of the Lord, and He will exalt you. (James 4:10)
You don't have to play the world's opportunistic game of politics. Let *Him* lift you up. Commit yourself to *His* authority and you'll have a sense of importance you've never known.

4. **Pleasure.** The last thread in Satan's web emphasizes sensuality and beauty. It starts when children are still in the nursery. Think of some of the classic stories parents read to their little ones: *The Ugly Duckling, Cinderella, Sleeping Beauty.* From the first years of our lives, it's instilled in us that this thing called beauty will bring the security of love. Scripture helps put our outward appearance in its proper place:
"For God sees not as man sees, for man looks at the outward appearance, but the Lord looks at the heart." (1 Sam. 16:7b)
Charm is deceitful and beauty is vain,
But a woman who fears the Lord, she shall be praised. (Prov. 31:30)

Avoiding Extremes

To beat an out-of-balance system that screams, blue-faced, "Get rich! Be popular! Take charge! Be beautiful!" some think it necessary to be equally extreme. They vow never to make a profit, to be a recluse, never to assume a leadership role, always to be plain. And instead of beating the world's system, they sometimes beat their opportunity to minister to others.

God hasn't called us to an ascetic lifestyle, but to a life of moderation—one in which we can best touch the world with the good news of Jesus and stimulate each other to love and good deeds (see Phil. 4:5, Heb. 10:24).

II. Truths for Believers to Remember

Because Satan will do anything to get us caught in his web, off-balance, we must keep four truths in the forefront of our minds.

A. We live in a world of opposing standards. The world's system and Christianity are constantly colliding, and the friction causes sparks that rival the electricity of even the most brilliant of lightning storms.

B. The world has an aggressive strategy. Society's strategy isn't passive or subtle. To those who are beautiful, intelligent, powerful, rich, or famous, rewards are lavishly given. Such people are lifted up, exalted, and made the pattern for all to follow.

C. We either adopt the world system or reject it. As Jesus says in Matthew's Gospel:

> "No one can serve two masters; for either he will hate the one and love the other, or he will hold to one and despise the other. You cannot serve God and mammon."[2] (6:24; see also James 4:4)

There's only room for one king on the throne of our hearts. And it's easy to see who we've chosen by the type of lives we lead.

D. If you reject it, you must do so with aggressiveness.

> Do not love the world, nor the things in the world. If anyone loves the world, the love of the Father is not in him. For all that is in the world, the lust of the flesh and the lust of the eyes and the boastful pride of life, is not from the Father, but is from the world. (1 John 2:15–16)

The pull to love the world is strong, unrelenting. To fight it requires more than whistling in the dark. It requires embracing a strength that only God can give.

> You are from God, little children, and have overcome them; because greater is He who is in you than he who is in the world. (4:4)

III. An Alternate Strategy for Believers

An English historian once wrote:

> Power tends to corrupt and absolute power corrupts absolutely.[3]

One of the Bible's most powerful men was Joshua. Successor to Moses, feared general, and leader of God's chosen nation, he had

---

2. In this passage, *mammon,* a common Aramaic word for riches, "merely means wealth, and is called 'unrighteous,' because the abuse of riches is more frequent than their right use.... Wealth, Jesus teaches, does not really belong to men, but as stewards they may use wealth prudently unto their eternal advantage. Instead of serving God and mammon alike we may serve God by the use of wealth, and thus lay up treasures for ourselves in heaven." From *The International Standard Bible Encyclopaedia,* vol. 3, ed. James Orr (1956; reprint, Grand Rapids, Mich.: William B. Eerdmans Publishing Co., 1976), pp. 1972–73.

3. Lord Acton, *Bartlett's Familiar Quotations,* 14th ed., rev. and enl., ed. Emily Morison Beck (Boston, Mass.: Little, Brown and Co., 1968), p. 750.

every opportunity to let his power become poisonous. But because his ultimate trust rested in the Lord, his power was purifying—godly and wise. In Joshua 24:13–15, we'll look at the words of this ancient leader and find an alternate strategy—one that will beat the baneful system of the world.

A. Recognize the Lord God as supreme. The Lord heaped His blessings upon the children of Israel; therefore, they were to serve Him as the one true God.

> " 'And I gave you a land on which you had not labored, and cities which you had not built, and you have lived in them; you are eating of vineyards and olive groves which you did not plant.' *Now, therefore, fear the Lord and serve Him in sincerity and truth."*
> (vv. 13–14a, emphasis added)

Clandestinely tucked in the pocket of this passage are four secrets to our aggressive strategy.

1. **Fear the Lord.** The command to fear the Lord doesn't mean that we should be afraid of Him, but that we should hold Him in reverence. The enemy of reverence is cynicism, which raises its bloated head in the form of sarcastic comments about the sacred Lord.

2. **Serve the Lord.** The Lord also commands us to be active and involved in His work. The enemy of service is passivity, which strips us of our motivation to do good and clothes us with a yawning, here-we-go-again attitude that keeps us away from our neighbors and churches, sitting at home in front of the TV.

3. **Sincerity.** We are to serve Him honestly, sincerely, without a trace of hypocrisy.

4. **Truth.** And finally, we need to be grounded in the truths of God's Word. In the fight against the world's system, there's no place for ignorance. Study His Word. Memorize it. Hide it in the clefts of your heart (Ps. 119:11).

A Rut Is Just a Grave with the Ends Kicked Out

You've met them. Sarcastic, cynical believers who know more theological terms than a seminary grad, yet are bitter and cold. The Lord isn't supreme in their lives. They're stuck in a rut. Their language is thriving, but their love has long since died.

Learn from these travesties of the faith. Keep your time with God creative and fresh. Keep your love alive![4]

---

4. For some help in keeping your spiritual love life fresh and alive, see *Restoring Your Spiritual Passion,* by Gordon MacDonald (Nashville, Tenn.: Thomas Nelson Publishers, 1986).

B. Reject all opposing philosophy. In order to beat the system, not only must we hold the Lord supreme, but we must also reject every semblance of worldly philosophies. As Joshua commanded Israel,

> "And put away the gods which your fathers served beyond the River and in Egypt, and serve the Lord." (Josh. 24:14b)

It won't necessarily be easy. Some of society's ways have become so deeply ingrained in our lives that we hardly recognize them as worldly. The best way to get them to surface is to ask yourself these searching questions: Who's glory am I doing this for? Why do I spend my time doing this? Does this activity buttress or batter my faith? Does this person help or hinder my walk?

C. Realize that others may not agree with you. It's not important that everyone else on the block sees things the way you do. What *is* important is that you know for yourself what's right and that you do it, wholeheartedly. Joshua challenges the Israelites to solidify their commitment to God with these words:

> "And if it is disagreeable in your sight to serve the Lord, choose for yourselves today whom you will serve: whether the gods which your fathers served which were beyond the River, or the gods of the Amorites in whose land you are living." (v. 15a)

D. Repeat and review your standard often. As if he hadn't made a strong enough statement, Joshua emphatically repeats his standard to the children of Israel.

> "But as for me and my house, we will serve the Lord." (v. 15b)

What kinds of messages do your children receive? Mixed among "Don't slam the door . . . make your bed . . . be nice to your sister," are there a few that remind them to "Memorize God's Word . . . love Him supremely . . . trust Him completely"? These are the standards that will echo in the chambers of their minds long after they leave the protective walls of your home.

IV. Biblical Warnings for the Heart

If we practice the strategy laid out in this lesson, we'll have what it takes to avoid the snare of the world's sticky web. But lest we think we can perfect this plan with an abracadabra attitude, let's consider a few warnings that will steep our strategy in reality.

A. It won't be easy, and it won't be sudden. It'll take time. And it'll take effort. But like housework, catching up is harder than keeping up. If we let the dust of our worldly habits build up, it will take a lot of elbow grease to clean and polish our philosophies. But with discipline, it won't be long until God's system, rich and pure as mahogany, will shine in our lives.

B. Your main problem will be inconsistency. After a study like this one, it's easy to get fired up and make big plans to fly wide of the world's web. But soon, daily routine sets in and steals most of the passion away, leaving us with just a flicker of conviction to change. The key to making this strategy a reality in your life is to fight hard for it—daily—even when the fire has waned.

C. If you don't start now, you never will. Procrastination will kill even the deepest conviction. Act on your desire to beat the world's system. Do it today . . . tomorrow never comes.

 Living Insights

Study One

The opposition lies in wait to pounce on our greatest areas of vulnerability. Therefore, let's study a little more about how to keep up our guard.

• As you read through Joshua 24:13–15, write down the verbs you see throughout the passage. Then, using the context, other Scriptures, and dictionaries, write out a definition for these action words.

Joshua 24:13–15	
Verbs	Definitions

Continued on next page

Verbs	Definitions

 Living Insights

Study Two ▬▬▬▬▬▬▬▬▬▬▬▬▬▬▬▬▬▬▬▬▬▬▬▬▬▬▬▬▬▬▬▬▬▬▬

There are so many practical truths in this study. It might be a wise idea to bring together a group of family or friends to sit down and discuss how these apply to your own situations. Use the following questions as a framework for your discussion.

- What specifics have you observed about the world's opposing standards?

- How does the world show its aggressiveness?

- How can you develop an equally aggressive strategy against the world?

- What's involved in recognizing that the Lord is supreme?

- Why is it difficult to reject other philosophies and to stand alone?

Books for Probing Further

Every good father disciplines with a hand both tough and tender. These qualities give a child the needed balance between an unbending standard to live by and an endless storehouse of grace. In our study of 1 Corinthians, we've seen a perfect example of this kind of relationship in the way Paul spiritually fathered the prideful congregation at Corinth.

First, Paul took the Corinthians straight to the woodshed, where his words stung their consciences like a wooden paddle put to their backsides (1 Cor. 1:1–6:11). Then he sat them down for a look-me-in-the-eyes chat, giving them practical advice for staying out of trouble (6:12–11:34). Finally, he gathered the Corinthian believers close to himself, answering their questions and embracing them with words of warm acceptance and grace (12:1–16:24).

Perhaps as you studied this letter you felt your heavenly Father's firm hand of correction on you for areas of sin in your life. If you did, we hope you've also felt His tender hand of forgiveness. His rebukes for straying from truth are strong. Yet His calm call to come back to the shelter of obedience is just as sure. To help sharpen your ears to His call of grace, we recommend the following books.

Coleman, Robert E. *The Master Plan of Discipleship.* Old Tappan, N.J.: Fleming H. Revell Co., 1987. In this book, the author examines the Acts of the Apostles to determine the heartbeat of evangelism—discipleship. While specific procedures of evangelism change with time, the principles God gave in the Great Commission have remained the same since they first left the Lord's lips (see Matt. 28:18–20).

Colson, Charles. *Loving God.* Grand Rapids, Mich.: Zondervan Publishing House, 1983. With a style that irresistibly tugs the reader forward, Colson explains what loving God entails. Powerful and moving, this book gives a faith-igniting challenge to radical obedience and commitment to God.

Gangel, Kenneth O. *Unwrap Your Spiritual Gifts.* Wheaton, Ill.: Victor Books, 1983. An excellent, thorough treatment of the subject of spiritual gifts, this book will help you discover which gifts you have and how you can best use them to serve the Body of Christ.

MacArthur, John F., Jr. *The Charismatics.* Grand Rapids, Mich.: Zondervan Publishing House, 1978. MacArthur presents the charismatic movement sensitively and thoroughly, measuring its tenets by the yardstick of scriptural truth. More than a cold, intellectual study of charismatic issues, this book will encourage you to maintain a warm, vital relationship with God.

McDowell, Josh. *The Resurrection Factor.* San Bernardino, Calif.: Here's Life Publishers, 1981. Josh McDowell, well-known apologist and author of *Evidence That Demands a Verdict,* examines the historical facts of Christ's Resurrection and shows how this miraculous event gives power to our lives today. McDowell provides a solid foundation for a well thought-out faith and excites a sure hope in our reliable Lord.

Ryrie, Charles C. *The Final Countdown.* Revised edition. Wheaton, Ill.: Victor Books, 1982. Here Ryrie explains the Bible's God-revealed prophecies that show us we can be confident in the face of confusion, find comfort in times of sorrow, and feel free to share with others the good news of God's healing forgiveness.

Sproul, R. C. *One Holy Passion: The Consuming Thirst to Know God.* Nashville, Tenn.: Thomas Nelson, 1987. As we saw in our study, the Corinthians were consumed with themselves; they thirsted to *know,* but they didn't thirst to *know God.* This left them puffed up, without love for God or each other. In his book, Sproul addresses this same issue in our lives, sparking in us a holy passion to know God—which should be the goal of every Christian's life.

Stedman, Ray C. *Body Life.* Second edition. Glendale, Calif.: Regal Books, 1972. This book was the first to educate our generation on how exercising spiritual gifts can bring life to the local church. Its truths still stand strong, challenging us to view ourselves and our gifts as irreplaceable to the whole body.

Walvoord, John F. *The Rapture Question.* Grand Rapids, Mich.: Zondervan Publishing House, 1957. Written by the former president of Dallas Theological Seminary, this book offers scriptural and comprehensive answers to questions about the Rapture of the Church. In the preface the author states his purpose well: "This study is offered in the spirit of strengthening the hope of those who love His appearing."

Acknowledgments

Insight for Living is grateful for permission to quote from the following source:

The Living Bible. Wheaton, Ill.: Tyndale House Publishers, 1971.

Insight for Living
Cassette Tapes
CALM ANSWERS FOR A CONFUSED CHURCH
A STUDY OF 1 CORINTHIANS 12–16

No one realized more than Paul the crippling effect of hard questions left unanswered. He tackles some of these tough issues in the final portion of his letter to the Corinthian church, providing strong, timely, yet compassionate answers for many questions that still trouble God's family today. Woven throughout this final segment of 1 Corinthians are the great themes of unity, assurance, hope, and most of all . . . love.

			U.S.	Canada
CAC	CS	Cassette series—includes album cover	$44.50	$56.50
		Individual cassettes—include messages		
		A and B	5.00	6.35

These prices are effective as of April 1988 and are subject to change without notice.

CAC 1-A: *One Head, One Body, Many Functions*—1 Corinthians 12:1–11
B: *Analogies from Anatomy*—1 Corinthians 12:12–31a

CAC 2-A: *Love: The Greatest of All*—1 Corinthians 13
B: *What about Tongues in the Church Today?*—1 Corinthians 14:1–25

CAC 3-A: *An Answer to Confusion about Tongues*—1 Corinthians 14:26–40
B: *Back from the Dead!*—1 Corinthians 15:1–11

CAC 4-A: *What If There Were No Resurrection?*—1 Corinthians 15:12–19
B: *Christ's Unfinished Work*—1 Corinthians 15:20–28

CAC 5-A: *Living for Tomorrow, Today*—1 Corinthians 15:29–34
B: *Our Future Bodies*—1 Corinthians 15:35–49

CAC 6-A: *The Greatest Mystery Ever Told*—1 Corinthians 15:50–58
B: *"Now Concerning the Collection"*—1 Corinthians 16:1–4

CAC 7-A: *ABCs of One-on-One*—1 Corinthians 16:5–12
B: *With All My Love . . . Paul*—1 Corinthians 16:13–20

CAC 8-A: *Anathema! Maranatha! Amen!*—1 Corinthians 16:21–24
B: *Standing Alone When Opposed**—Joshua 24:13–15

*This message was not a part of the original series but is compatible with it.

How to Order by Mail

Ordering is easy and convenient. Simply mark on the order form whether you want the series or individual tapes, including the quantity you desire. Tear out the order form and mail it with your payment to the appropriate address on the bottom of the form. We will process your order as promptly as we can.

United States orders: If you wish your order to be shipped first-class for faster delivery, please add 10 percent of the total order amount (not including California sales tax). Otherwise, please allow four to six weeks for delivery by fourth-class mail. We accept personal checks, money orders, Visa, and Master-Card in payment for materials. Unfortunately, we are unable to offer invoicing or COD orders.

Canadian orders: Please add 7 percent of your total order for first-class postage and allow approximately four weeks for delivery. For our listeners in British Columbia, a 6 percent sales tax must also be added to the total of all tape orders (not including postage). For further information, please contact our office at (604) 272-5811. We accept personal checks, money orders, Visa, or MasterCard in payment for materials. Unfortunately, we are unable to offer invoicing or COD orders.

Overseas orders: If you live outside the United States or Canada, please allow six to ten weeks for delivery by surface mail. If you would like your order sent airmail, the delivery time may be reduced. Whether you choose surface or airmail delivery, postage costs must be added to the amount of purchase and included with your order. Please use the following chart to determine the correct postage. Due to fluctuating currency rates, we can accept only personal checks made payable in U.S. funds, international money orders, Visa, or MasterCard in payment for materials.

Type of Postage	Cassettes
Surface	10% of total order
Airmail	25% of total order

For Faster Service, Order by Telephone

To purchase using Visa or MasterCard, you are welcome to use our **toll-free** number between the hours of 8:30 A.M. and 4:00 P.M., Pacific time, Monday through Friday. The number is **1-800-772-8888,** and it may be used anywhere in the United States except California, Hawaii, and Alaska. Telephone orders from these states and overseas are handled through our Sales Department at (714) 870-9161. Canadian residents should call (604) 272-5811. We are unable to accept collect calls.

Our Guarantee

Our cassettes are guaranteed for ninety days against faulty performance or breakage due to a defect in the tape. For best results, please be sure your tape recorder is in good operating condition and is cleaned regularly.

Note: To cover processing and handling, there is a $10 fee for *any* returned check.

Order Form

CAC CS represents the entire *Calm Answers for a Confused Church* series, while CAC 1–8 are the individual tapes included in the series.

Series or Tape	Unit Price U.S.	Canada	Quantity	Amount
CAC CS	$44.50	$56.50		$
CAC 1	5.00	6.35		
CAC 2	5.00	6.35		
CAC 3	5.00	6.35		
CAC 4	5.00	6.35		
CAC 5	5.00	6.35		
CAC 6	5.00	6.35		
CAC 7	5.00	6.35		
CAC 8	5.00	6.35		
Subtotal				
Sales tax *6% for orders delivered in California or British Columbia*				
Postage *7% in Canada; overseas residents see "How to Order by Mail"*				
10% optional first-class shipping and handling *U.S. residents only*				
Gift to Insight for Living *Tax-deductible in the U.S. and Canada*				
Total amount due *Please do not send cash.*			$	

If there is a balance: ☐ apply it as a donation ☐ please refund

Form of payment:

☐ Check or money order made payable to Insight for Living

☐ Credit card (circle one):   Visa   MasterCard

Card Number _____ Expiration Date _____

Signature _____
We cannot process your credit card purchase without your signature.

Name _____

Address _____

City _____

State/Province _____ Zip/Postal Code _____

Country _____

Telephone ( ) _____ Radio Station ___ ___ ___ ___
If questions arise concerning your order, we may need to contact you.

Mail this order form to the Sales Department at one of these addresses:
Insight for Living, Post Office Box 4444, Fullerton, CA 92634
Insight for Living Ministries, Post Office Box 2510, Vancouver, BC, Canada V6B 3W7

INSIGHT FOR LIVING

Broadcast Schedule

May 11–June 29, 1988

Family Talks

Wednesday	**May 11**	**Plain Talk—The People**
Thursday	**May 12**	Just as he did during the Family Talks
Friday	**May 13**	that aired after part one of his study in
		1 Corinthians, Chuck Swindoll will join some
		of his associates in ministry to reflect on part
Monday	**May 16**	two, *Practical Helps for a Hurting Church.* This

time they'll look at the issues of personal
holiness, singleness and marriage, rights and
responsibilities, and public worship. Chances
are the tough questions they discuss will be
the same ones your church wrestles with too.

Calm Answers for a Confused Church
A Study of 1 Corinthians 12–16

Tuesday	**May 17**	**One Head, One Body, Many Functions**
		1 Corinthians 12:1–11
Wednesday	**May 18**	**One Head, One Body, Many Functions**
Thursday	**May 19**	**Analogies from Anatomy**
		1 Corinthians 12:12–31a
Friday	**May 20**	**Analogies from Anatomy**

Monday	**May 23**	**Love: The Greatest of All**
		1 Corinthians 13
Tuesday	**May 24**	**Love: The Greatest of All**

Wednesday	May 25	**What about Tongues in the Church Today?** 1 Corinthians 14:1–25
Thursday	May 26	**What about Tongues in the Church Today?**
Friday	May 27	**An Answer to Confusion about Tongues** 1 Corinthians 14:26–40
Monday	May 30	**An Answer to Confusion about Tongues**
Tuesday	May 31	**Back from the Dead!** 1 Corinthians 15:1–11
Wednesday	June 1	**Back from the Dead!**
Thursday	June 2	**What If There Were No Resurrection?** 1 Corinthians 15:12–19
Friday	June 3	**What If There Were No Resurrection?**
Monday	June 6	**Christ's Unfinished Work** 1 Corinthians 15:20–28
Tuesday	June 7	**Christ's Unfinished Work**
Wednesday	June 8	**Living for Tomorrow, Today** 1 Corinthians 15:29–34
Thursday	June 9	**Living for Tomorrow, Today**
Friday	June 10	**Our Future Bodies** 1 Corinthians 15:35–49
Monday	June 13	**Our Future Bodies**
Tuesday	June 14	**The Greatest Mystery Ever Told** 1 Corinthians 15:50–58
Wednesday	June 15	**The Greatest Mystery Ever Told**
Thursday	June 16	**"Now Concerning the Collection"** 1 Corinthians 16:1–4
Friday	June 17	**"Now Concerning the Collection"**
Monday	June 20	**ABCs of One-on-One** 1 Corinthians 16:5–12
Tuesday	June 21	**ABCs of One-on-One**
Wednesday	June 22	**With All My Love . . . Paul** 1 Corinthians 16:13–20
Thursday	June 23	**With All My Love . . . Paul**
Friday	June 24	**Anathema! Maranatha! Amen!** 1 Corinthians 16:21–24
Monday	June 27	**Anathema! Maranatha! Amen!**
Tuesday	June 28	**Standing Alone When Opposed** Joshua 24:13–15
Wednesday	June 29	**Standing Alone When Opposed**

CALM ANSWERS FOR A CONFUSED CHURCH
SPECIAL BOOK OFFER

Throughout 1 Corinthians, Paul writes about problems in the Corinthian church, problems that infiltrate our churches as well. As he winds up this powerful letter, the apostle softens his approach, encouraging the church to bond together and reach out to others with the love God has shown them. "Therefore, my dear brothers, stand firm. Let nothing move you. Always give yourselves fully to the work of the Lord, because you know that your labor in the Lord is not in vain" (1 Cor. 15:58, NIV). To help you follow Paul's counsel, we are pleased to offer these three books.

The Church Is Not for Perfect People. William Murray, son of outspoken atheist Madalyn Murray O'Hair, grew up without God or morals. At thirty-three, he found Christ and attended church for the first time. In this book, Murray speaks candidly to Christians about accepting and helping people like him who enter church burdened with a sinful past.

Improving Your Serve. Becoming a caring body of believers requires change from within, a relinquishing of self. With his practical, to-the-point style, Chuck Swindoll shows us how to develop the art of unselfish living. Only then will we demonstrate God's command to model Christ, who "did not come to be served, but to serve" (Mark 10:45, NASB).

Who Speaks for God? In this hard-hitting book, Charles Colson challenges the church to confront the world with real Christianity—giving, forgiving, serving, loving. Each of these chapters was first published as a monthly column in Prison Fellowship's newsletter. Every one will compel you to make a difference in the lives of the hurting people around you.

ORDER FORM

These books are available for the following prices:

Title	U.S.	Canada
The Church Is Not for Perfect People (softcover)	$6.95	$ 9.95
Improving Your Serve (softcover)	3.50	5.10
Who Speaks for God? (softcover)	7.95	11.50

Special multibook discount: You can order all three of these books for only $16.00 in the U.S., which saves you $2.40 off the regular price, and just $22.00 in Canada, for a savings of $4.55.

This special book offer expires August 15, 1988.

Book	Price	Quantity	Amount
☐ *The Church Is Not for Perfect People*	$ _____	_____	$ _____
☐ *Improving Your Serve*	$ _____	_____	$ _____
☐ *Who Speaks for God?*	$ _____	_____	$ _____

Deduct for multibook discount $ _____

Subtotal $ _____

If your order is delivered in
California, please add 6 percent sales tax $ _____

For faster shipping, U.S. residents can add
10 percent for first-class shipping and handling $ _____

Canadian residents add 7 percent for postage $ _____

Contribution to the Insight for Living radio ministry $ _____
All contributions are tax-deductible.

Total Amount Enclosed $ _____

Check or money order should be made payable to Insight for Living.

Credit card purchases:

☐ Visa ☐ MasterCard Number _____

Expiration Date _____

Signature _____
We cannot process your credit card purchase without your signature.

You are welcome to use our toll-free number (for Visa and MasterCard orders only) between the hours of 8:30 A.M. and 4:00 P.M., Pacific time, Monday through Friday. The number is **(800) 772-8888.** This number may be used anywhere in the United States except Alaska, California, and Hawaii. To order from these areas, call our Sales Department at (714) 870-9161. To order from Canada, call (604) 272-5811.

Name _____

Address _____

City _____

State/Province _____ Zip/Postal Code _____

Country _____

Telephone (____) _____ Radio Station ___ ___ ___ ___

If questions arise concerning your order, we may need to contact you.

Insight for Living • Post Office Box 4444, Fullerton, CA 92634
Insight for Living Ministries • Post Office Box 2510, Vancouver, BC, Canada V6B 3W7

Please allow four to six weeks for delivery.